# Tolstoy on Aesthetics
## What is art?

H.O. MOUNCE
*University of Wales,
Swansea, UK*

LONDON AND NEW YORK

First published 2001 by Ashgate Publishing

Reissued 2019 by Routledge
2 Park Square, Milton Park, Abingdon, Oxon, OX14 4RN
605 Third Avenue, New York, NY 10017

First issued in paperback 2021

*Routledge is an imprint of the Taylor & Francis Group, an informa business*

Copyright © H. O. Mounce 2001

The author has asserted his moral right under the Copyright, Designs and Patents Act, 1988, to be identified as the author of this work.

All rights reserved. No part of this book may be reprinted or reproduced or utilised in any form or by any electronic, mechanical, or other means, now known or hereafter invented, including photocopying and recording, or in any information storage or retrieval system, without permission in writing from the publishers.

Notice:
Product or corporate names may be trademarks or registered trademarks, and are used only for identification and explanation without intent to infringe.

Publisher's Note
The publisher has gone to great lengths to ensure the quality of this reprint but points out that some imperfections in the original copies may be apparent.

Disclaimer
The publisher has made every effort to trace copyright holders and welcomes correspondence from those they have been unable to contact.

A Library of Congress record exists under LC control number:

ISBN 13: 978-1-138-70329-2 (hbk)
ISBN 13: 978-1-315-20322-5 (ebk)
ISBN 13: 978-1-138-63107-6 (pbk)

In memory
of
Dick Beardsmore

# TOLSTOY ON AESTHETICS

Tolstoy's view of art is discussed in most courses in aesthetics, particularly his main text *What is Art?* He believed that the importance of art lies not in its purely aesthetic qualities but in its connection with life, and that art becomes decadent where this connection is lost. This view has often been misconceived and its strength overlooked.

This book presents a clear exposition of Tolstoy's *What is Art?*, highlighting the value and importance of Tolstoy's views in relation to aesthetics. Howard Mounce considers the problems which exercised Tolstoy and explains their fundamental importance in contemporary disputes. Having viewed these problems of aesthetics as they arise in a classic work, Mounce affords readers fresh insights not simply into the problems of aesthetics themselves, but also into their contemporary treatment. Students and interested readers of aesthetics and philosophy, as well as those exploring the works of Tolstoy in literature, will find this book of particular interest and will discover that reading *What is Art?* with attention affords something of the excitement found in removing grime from an oil painting – gradually, from underneath, there appears an authentic masterpiece.

# Contents

Preface — vii

1. The Background — 1
2. Art and Society — 13
3. The Problem — 18
4. The Central Features — 24
5. Art and Morality — 29
6. Art in History — 34
7. Decadent Art — 40
8. Wagner — 49
9. Summary and Elaboration — 65
10. Alternative Theories — 76
11. Shakespeare — 94

Afterword — 108
Bibliography — 109
Index — 110

# Preface

Tolstoy believed that the importance of art lies not in its purely aesthetic qualities but in its connection with life, and that it becomes decadent when that connection is lost. This view has often been misconceived and its strength overlooked. My purpose is to correct the conventional view by giving a clear exposition of what Tolstoy really meant.

Students of aesthetics who are primarily interested in *What is Art?*, Tolstoy's main work in aesthetics, may wish to concentrate on Chapters 3, 4, 5, 6, 7, 8 and 10. They will there find a detailed exposition of the work, chapter by chapter. My exposition is critical where this is appropriate but my chief aim has been to bring out what is valuable and important in the work.

The more general reader who is primarily interested in Tolstoy as a man and as a thinker will find in the first two chapters an account of his life and of the background to his thought. Chapter 9 presents a detailed case study of the type of art to which Tolstoy is opposed. Since I believe that my work will be of interest to students of literature, I have concluded with a chapter on Tolstoy's famous view of Shakespeare. This view has often been criticized – for example, by George Orwell – as the result of prejudice. I show that this criticism is mistaken. Even those who disagree with Tolstoy's view can learn much about Shakespeare by studying it closely.

Student and general reader alike will discover that reading *What is Art?* with attention affords something of the excitement found in removing the grime from an old painting. Gradually, from underneath, there appears an authentic masterpiece.

Peter Lewis, Catherine Osborne, Ian Robinson and Carola Sandbacka have read this work, whether in whole or in part, when it was in manuscript. My thanks are due to them for their helpful advice. My thanks are due also to Helen Baldwin, who prepared the work for publication.

L. Tolstoy, taken from A. N. Wilson, *Tolstoy*, London, Hamish Hamilton, 1988, between pp. 386 and 387.

CHAPTER ONE

# The Background

Tolstoy's *What is Art?* is a work that writers in aesthetics often note but rarely study with sympathy. It was written after his religious conversion, when he repudiated much of his earlier life, including his work as an artist. This is considered eccentric, and the explanation for his eccentricity – or so it is thought – lies ready to hand in his religious conversion. It belongs to the mythology of intellectual life in the present century that if a man takes to religion, he thereby sacrifices his talent. 'Reading the reminiscences of Tolstoy,' said D. H. Lawrence, 'one can only feel shame at the way Tolstoy denied all that was good in him, with vehement cowardice. He degraded himself infinitely, he perjured himself far worse than did Peter when he denied Christ. Peter repented.'[1] Lawrence here expresses, in an extreme form, views which are widely held. Tolstoy's greatness as a writer is not denied. But it is found in the two masterpieces of his earlier period, *War and Peace* and *Anna Karenina*. The later works may be discounted and, along with them, *What is Art?*

Now it will be important, at the start, to remove the above prejudice. After his conversion, Tolstoy was as prolific in his writings as he was before. For example, during this period he wrote *The Death of Ivan Ilyich, Resurrection, The Kreutzer Sonata, The Devil, Master and Man, Father Sergius, The Forged Coupon, After the Ball* and *Hadji Murat*. Most of these are masterpieces, the last being perhaps the most perfect short novel ever written. During this period he wrote also a host of parables which were modelled on those of the Gospels and which are unsurpassed in secular literature. In addition, he wrote numerous works dealing with social and religious problems, some of which – for example, the famous *Confession* – are themselves literary masterpieces. Those who suppose that Tolstoy sacrificed his talent to religious moralizing might give their attention to *The Forged Coupon*. This story traces the consequences for evil of a forged note as it passes from hand to hand. At a certain point goodness enters the story and its consequences are contrasted with those of evil. The work is certainly didactic, indeed overtly religious. It is also a marvel of narrative economy. The characters are more numerous than one finds in the average novel; every one is alive and Tolstoy handles them all within eighty pages. It is the work of a supreme master. Had Tolstoy never written *War and Peace* and *Anna Karenina*, the work he produced in his later years would still have entitled him to a place amongst the greatest writers of his century.

It is true that *What is Art?* may be an exception. Even though he retained his power as an artist, Tolstoy might still have been foolish when he talked about art. It is possible; but it is not likely. For *What is Art?* is not the product of momentary impatience or a fit of irritation but of prolonged reflection. The ideas contained in the work were first sketched some fifteen years before it appeared. Tolstoy continually reworked them until he had given them a form which satisfied him. In these circumstances it would be remarkable if they contained nothing of interest. Indeed, if that were so, it would itself make the work interesting. For we should then have the intriguing problem of how a man who had practised an art with supreme mastery nevertheless had nothing useful to say about it.

Nor need we be too impressed by the criticisms of those who disparage the book, for they fall into a familiar pattern. We may take as an instance the criticisms advanced by Henri Troyat, in his celebrated biography of Tolstoy.[2] His references to Tolstoy's view on art are intermittent and invariably disparaging. On his view, Tolstoy was advocating an extreme form of didacticism, according to which the value of art depends not on its aesthetic qualities but wholly on its moral content. We may note here a certain kinship with the prejudice we have just exposed. It is assumed that since Tolstoy sacrificed his talent to religious moralizing, he was bound to value art for its moral content rather than its aesthetic qualities. In fact Troyat's interpretation is in conflict with Tolstoy's explicit view. One of his main points in *What is Art?* is that no art has value, whatever its content, unless it has what he calls 'infectiousness'. He illustrates what he means by the example of a boy who vividly recreates for an audience his experience of encountering a wolf. It is obvious that this ability, which Tolstoy takes as essential to the artistic process, can be identified in an artist without one's *approving* of what he conveys.

It is obvious also that Tolstoy did not identify moral content with explicit moralizing. In this respect, he did himself a disservice, through faulty judgement, in *What is Art?* when he chose examples to illustrate the best types of art. Some of his examples are didactic in a bad sense. The passage is a favourite one with his critics, for it fits their preconceptions, few of them, for example, failing to quote *Uncle Tom's Cabin*. In this, they ignore Tolstoy's explicit statement that what he has chosen are mere examples of his view, which are of no intrinsic importance, for those who agree with his view but disagree with his examples may choose better ones for themselves. The view itself in no way implies that the best art should moralize. Indeed it is evident, if one reads him with attention, that Tolstoy did not identify moral content with paraphrasable content, nor yet with conscious moral intention. For him, the moral content of a work did not consist in some element which might be extracted from the work itself but in the attitude which pervades it. Moreover, the attitude which pervades it need not have been consciously intended by the artist himself. The point is evident in his praise for Chekhov's *Darling*. Tolstoy particularly valued this story because he believed that it had arisen from Chekhov's artistic instinct rather than from his conscious purpose. On Tolstoy's view, Chekhov had intended when he began the story to satirize its heroine but he had ended by making her lovable. The point is even more evident in his essay on Maupassant, for it forms the very burden of the essay. Tolstoy held that Maupassant was a genuine artist whose attitudes to life had a corrupting effect on his art. The point of the essay, however, is to show that in his best work Maupassant transcends those attitudes, so that the attitudes which pervade his best work are in conflict with those he explicitly held.

*What is Art?* exhibits the supreme virtue of Tolstoy's later work. Repeatedly in his later work he raises a question which goes to the heart of the matter that concerns him, refuses to leave that question until he has found a satisfactory answer and then conveys it to his audience with unsurpassed clarity. It is remarkable how often the question turns out to be one that has occurred to all of us but which we have been afraid to express in case we make fools of ourselves. In this respect Tolstoy was entirely fearless. Sometimes he does make a fool of himself. For the question once raised turns out to rest on a prejudice. But we are better all the same for getting it into the open. The book has its faults. But one can learn more from Tolstoy when he is wrong than from most authors when they are right.

Before dealing with the book in detail, we must set it against the background of Tolstoy's life. He was born on the 28 August 1828, at the family estate of Yasnaya Polyana, the grandson of Prince Volkonsky, a former military commander and ambassador to the King of Prussia. In 1800, for reasons which remain unclear, the Prince withdrew from public life and retired to his estate, where he remained until his death some twenty years later. In the Prince's day, Yasnaya Polyana had the qualities in miniature of a feudal state. The gate was guarded, night and day, by two armed sentinels. Every morning, at seven o'clock, a group of musicians, gathered from amongst his serfs, assembled beneath the Prince's bedroom window and awakened him to the sound of music. Gorky records that Tolstoy, late in life, when he mended his own shoes and dressed in a peasant's blouse, would sometimes startle his visitors, if he considered them impertinent or condescending, by suddenly revealing the bearing and authority of an aristocrat.[3]

He had something else in common with his grandfather. The Prince was a devotee of the Enlightenment, a friend of reason, an enemy of superstition. His favourite reading was in the French Encyclopaedists. He was followed in this by his grandson. The thinkers of the Enlightenment saw in history a progress from darkness into comparative light. The cause of darkness, they thought, was chiefly mystification, perpetuated by priests in the interests of the wealthy and powerful. The cure for mystification lay in the clarity of reason, it being axiomatic amongst them that any belief should be dismissed as mystification which could not be made entirely clear. It followed for them that the corruptions of the past, being largely the product of conspiracy, were not inherent in human nature. It is in the institutions imposed on human nature, not in human nature itself, that evil lies. Tolstoy absorbed these attitudes at an early age and they became engrained in his mind. We shall find in *What is Art?*, for example, that he attributes the corruptions of art entirely to the wealthy and powerful and takes for granted that simple people are free from those corruptions, that he links the best art with the most *progressive* form of religion and that the mark of a progressive religion is its comparative freedom from theology and dogma, these being forms of mystification, the product of priestcraft.

The influence of the Enlightenment is seen also in Tolstoy's treatment of his opponents. As his critics remark, in dealing with his opponents he is often impatient and sometimes unfair. Here he did himself a disservice. For his critics infer from his treatment of his opponents that his own views are the product of mere bias. Nothing could be further from the truth. Tolstoy's views are almost invariably the product of prolonged study and reflection. This is true, as we shall see, even where he holds a view, such as his view of Shakespeare, which at first sight seems outrageous. He had the true thinker's inability to accept a view until he had made it entirely clear to his mind. Once he is convinced, however, it is a different matter. All hesitation disappears. Confronted by opposition, he charges. The reason is that, like the thinkers of the Enlightenment, he easily believed that opposition to the truth arises not so much from honest error as from *mystification*. Behind such opposition, he was only too ready to assume, there lies some sinister interest concerned not to reveal but to obscure the truth. Isaiah Berlin has remarked that Tolstoy's faults are really the opposite of those which his critics attribute to him.[4] No one, for example, was less inclined than Tolstoy to be attracted by impractical and muddle-headed mysticism. It would be more plausible to accuse him of being unduly influenced by those thinkers who in the eighteenth century devoted themselves exclusively to reason.

Prince Volkonsky's only child Marya was unmarried at his death. In her thirties she married a handsome but impoverished nobleman, Nicholas Tolstoy. One might have suspected that the inducement, on his side, had something to do with his impoverishment. In fact, the marriage was a happy one. Leo was the fourth of their children, all of whom were boys. They had a fifth child, a daughter, but Marya died shortly after her birth. After the father's death, the family estates were divided amongst the children. The family home at Yasnaya Polyana was assigned to Leo. It remained his home throughout his life.

In his youth, Tolstoy had difficulty in fixing on a purpose in life. He attended the university at Kazan but left without taking a degree. In December 1850, his eldest brother Nicholas, who was serving with the Russian army in the Caucasus, returned home on leave. At the time Tolstoy had fallen into the habit of gambling and was losing money. Nicholas persuaded his brother to join him when he returned to his regiment. It was while serving in the Caucasus that Tolstoy published *Childhood*, his first work. The fault with most young writers is that they are primarily interested in themselves and constantly intrude themselves on their readers. It is only with effort and much practice that they learn to write more objectively. Tolstoy wrote in that way from the start. Vivid re-creation seems to have come to him by instinct. If one of his characters sits in a chair, one can see the chair as well as the character, and one can distinguish it from any other chair. He disappears, as it were, from the world he creates, so that his readers have the impression of seeing it for themselves. He was fortunate, also, in having his work readily appreciated. Nekrasov, the editor of a leading Russian journal, to whom the manuscript of *Childhood* was submitted, immediately recognized his talent.

In November 1854, Tolstoy was transferred to the Crimea. It was there that he wrote the most successful of his early works, the *Sevastopol Sketches*. He was present at the fall of Sevastopol and recorded his impressions as they occurred. Tolstoy is famous for his vivid re-creation of warfare. He acknowledged a debt to Stendhal, whose description of the battle of Waterloo in his *The Charterhouse of Parma* he had carefully studied. But Stendhal described the battle from a single viewpoint. Tolstoy achieved even greater realism by adopting a number of viewpoints, so that the battle of Sevastopol is seen, as it were, from many angles.

On his return to civilian life, Tolstoy was welcomed in intellectual circles as one of Russia's most promising writers. Turgenev was one of the first to welcome him. Their relationship, however, was stormy. As we shall find in *What is Art?*, Tolstoy was not impressed by intellectuals. As we shall also find, he was equally suspicious of his fellow aristocrats, so long as they confined themselves to court circles. The bourgeoisie, which at that time hardly existed in Russia, he did not know. His sympathies were confined to those who lived on the land, whether as landowner or peasant. The rest he viewed with suspicion. The point is of some importance in understanding his attitude to the art of the later nineteenth century, which, in his view, had become divorced from the values of the land. His sympathy with the peasants was exhibited when, at about the age of thirty, he established a village school. In education he was a follower of Rousseau. The aim was to develop children according to nature, not to stuff them with information. He did the teaching himself, though later employing assistants. The evidence is that he was a gifted teacher. It seems that he held the attention as readily with the spoken as with the written word. The gift remained with him. There are a number of photographs of him in old age talking to children. In each case, the children attend not to the camera but wholly to him.

Tolstoy married in 1862. His wife, Sonya Behrs, belonged to a family with whom he had long been acquainted. Their marriage is probably the most closely scrutinized in the whole of literary history. In the long run it brought them both great misery. But for many years they were happy together. The supreme artistic achievements of Tolstoy's later years were in the shorter literary forms, *Resurrection*, the one proper novel of the period, being of imperfect quality. His supreme achievements in the full novel, *War and Peace* and *Anna Karenina*, were produced during the first fifteen years of his marriage. His wife not only encouraged him but was an active helper in these achievements. Tolstoy was an inveterate rewriter, crossing out, inserting, scribbling in the margin. Nor did this process end with the arrival of the proofs. For these were subjected to the same process. Preparing a final manuscript in these circumstances was a daunting task. Sonya did most of this work, having the ability to decipher sentences which were illegible to Tolstoy himself.

*War and Peace* was written when Tolstoy was in his late thirties (1863–69), *Anna Karenina* when he was in his late forties (1873–77). At the age of fifty, he was a famous and wealthy man. It was at this time that he underwent the spiritual crisis which he recorded in *A Confession*, one of the masterpieces of religious literature.[5] The work is concerned with the most fundamental question: what is the meaning of life? The question has been raised often enough. But Tolstoy's concern with the question is not in the abstract. He invests it with the most intense personal urgency. Thus he describes himself, in his late forties, as oppressed with a sense of futility. What concerns him is not the significance of this or that activity within his life but the significance of his life as such. This activity has significance by leading to that one. But what about the life within which these activities occur? Where does that lead? It leads only to death. But how then can his life be of more than passing significance?

Tolstoy tried to find an answer to this question through an intensive study of the world's greatest thinkers. But this study served only to increase his sense of futility. On purely rational grounds there seems no answer to the question of what is the meaning of life. But then it occurs to him that the meaning of life may not depend on purely rational grounds. In order to gain faith in life, he is trying to prove that it has meaning. But perhaps the meaning of life becomes clear only to those who *already* have faith in it.

Where then can he find people who have faith in life? He thinks of the peasants who surround him on his estates. They are oppressed by many hardships but none is oppressed by the futility of life. They believe that life is a gift given them by God and that they should live according to his will not according to their own. Moreover when Tolstoy thinks of life in this way, he finds it has meaning for him also.

It may be noted that Tolstoy has shifted radically in his attitude to reason. The assumption of the Enlightenment, which Tolstoy had shared, was that it is only through reason that people can overcome superstition and stand in the right relation to the world. His view now, quite contrary to that of the Enlightenment, is that one cannot put oneself in the right relation to the world simply through reason. Rather, reason is fruitful only amongst those who *already* stand in the right relation to the world. Thus one cannot simply through reason prove that life has meaning and put oneself in the right relation to God and one's neighbour. It is only those who have the right attitude to God and their neighbour who have reason to believe that life has meaning. As we shall find, Tolstoy's attitude to art has a parallel in his attitude to reason. The central view in *What is Art?* is that art depends for its importance, even in its own sphere, on what transcends it. Thus it is devoid of significance so far as it is practised only for its own sake. It is through its relation to life, to what transcends it, that it has its importance. The function of art is to express what the whole being of man, will, heart and spirit, has experienced. It is valueless so far as it attempts to spin its purposes out of itself.[6]

But now there occurs a phenomenon which, at first sight, is somewhat puzzling. After his conversion, as one might have expected, Tolstoy returned to the Orthodox faith, attended church, and partook of the sacraments. But he soon became restive. With regard to the central sacrament, in what sense, precisely, does one partake of the body and blood of Christ? With regard to dogma, how can God be both three and one? With regard to the ritual of the Orthodox faith, is it really necessary? Does one find it, for example, in the Gospels? Tolstoy turned to the Gospels and submitted them to intensive study, learning Greek in order to study them in the original. A brilliant linguist, he acquired the language in a remarkably short time.

The conclusion of his study was that the religion of the Church is not the Christianity of the Gospels. Indeed worse: it is in conflict with genuine Christianity. In the Gospels we find no organized Church and no hierarchical division. Thus there are no distinctions amongst a priesthood – between archbishop, bishop and lesser clergy. In fact, there is no distinction between priesthood and laity. The followers of Christ are all simple men and they are all equal. Again, there is a complete repudiation of the world, by which is meant any form of life which involves the pursuit of wealth, power or social prestige. In the Gospels, no value whatever is placed on these things. Quite the contrary: it is better to be poor and insignificant, as judged by worldly standards. But in the religion of the Church hierarchical division, absent from the Gospels, is treated as an essential feature of Christianity. We find, too, that being a Christian is compatible with pursuing and occupying positions of wealth, power and prestige. We find, further, that belief in Christianity amounts to believing in the occurrence some two thousand years ago of certain miraculous or supernatural events, in accepting the dogmas of the Church and in following its ritual practices. Yet none of these things is genuine Christianity. Genuine Christianity is essentially simple: it consists in believing that the spirit of God is in all men and that we should love our neighbour as ourselves.

Now what is somewhat puzzling in Tolstoy's account of orthodox Christianity is that it is strikingly reminiscent of the account given by the thinkers of the Enlightenment, whose attitude in many of its essentials has been rejected. Roughly put, on his account, the history of Christianity is one of systematic corruption perpetuated by priests in the interest of the wealthy and powerful. That was roughly the attitude of Voltaire. We may note, also, Tolstoy's attitude to the miraculous or supernatural elements in Christianity. On his view, these are simply forms of mystification or superstition. Here again he proceeds in the manner of Voltaire. Tolstoy's defence against criticisms of this type was that faith transcends but is not incompatible with reason and that a true faith cannot demand a sacrifice of the intelligence. No doubt he is correct. But one would not have expected the intelligence, once enlightened by faith, to go on working in exactly the same way. For example, one might have expected it to find importance in factors hitherto neglected. A case in point is Tolstoy's attitude to miracles. The thinkers of the Enlightenment were determined in their attitude to miracles by their belief in the absolute truth of the Newtonian or mechanical system of the world. The absolute truth of that system may certainly be doubted. It is now rejected within physics itself. Here surely is an area within which an invigorated intelligence might exercise itself. In fact, Tolstoy's attitude is identical with that of the Enlightenment.

The phenomenon, however, is not as puzzling as it first appears. It may be explained by what William James called the *apperceptive mass*. He was referring to those assumptions, beliefs, tendencies, of which we are hardly conscious but which influence the way we experience the world. James employed the notion in criticism of eighteenth-century empiricism. He argued that knowledge cannot depend simply on sense experience, for what we experience depends on what we notice and that, in its turn, on our apperceptive mass, the assumptions we bring to our experience. The apperceptive mass is astonishingly resistant to change. Assumptions that are formed early in life tend to persist even when we have found in certain respects that they are erroneous. The point applies to Tolstoy. The principles of the Enlightenment formed part of his apperceptive mass and even when he had found them erroneous in important respects, they continued to influence him. We shall find their influence throughout *What is Art?*

It is important to note, however, that Tolstoy's account of Christianity has its strong side as well as its weak. It is weakest where it assumes that the whole of genuine Christianity must already be clearly expressed in the Gospels. Indeed that view is in conflict with the Gospels themselves. Christ himself says that his disciples have much to learn that will not become clear to them until after his death. It follows that genuine Christianity must include a *development* of truths contained in the Gospels. For example, the test of a dogma cannot be simply that it reproduces in the same form what the Gospels have already expressed. It may also make explicit what the Gospels contain only in an implicit form. There is a limit, however, to what can count as the development of a Christian doctrine. One idea cannot be the development of another if the first *contradicts* the second. Now here we come upon the strong side of Tolstoy's account. For he argues, often with great power, that certain beliefs and procedures in orthodox Christianity are in *conflict* with the truths of the Gospels.

To appreciate his argument, we need to consider what Tolstoy took to be the essential truths of the Gospels. He summarized them in a series of commandments.[7] These, roughly speaking, are that we should never resort to violence in any form, that we should aspire to complete chastity, that we should never swear an oath or take part in any form of institutional punishment and that we should love our enemies, this entailing that we should never give preference to our own nation over others. The practices of orthodox Christianity, at a number of points, seem evidently to be in conflict with these views. We may take as an instance the view that a Christian should aspire to complete chastity, that is to abstain from sexual relations. This is plainly in conflict with the view of some modern churchmen, who are anxious to affirm the essential holiness of those very relations. But it seems equally in conflict with the practice of Christianity: in most of its forms, marriage is treated as a sacrament. Tolstoy argued, with some force, that this practice is quite unscriptural. In the Gospels, marriage is affirmed only as a concession to human weakness.

Now I have said that we are dealing with the strong side of Tolstoy's account. To most of his critics, however, it is precisely this side which is the weakest. The general charge is that his views are quite impractical, making absurd demands on human nature. But his critics here assume that Tolstoy intended them as practical. They assume, in effect, that Christ's commands, as found, for example, in the Sermon on the Mount, are practical devices for making the world a better place. The objection to this interpretation is that the commands are impossible to satisfy. The point is evident in Christ's command to be perfect: 'Be ye perfect even as the Father in heaven is perfect.' One may deceive oneself into believing that one can satisfy some of Christ's commands, such as loving one's enemies. But only an idiot will believe that he can make himself perfect. Christ's commands are evidently not practical devices, relative to human capacity, for making things better. They are judgements of absolute value against which one may measure one's capacities – only to find them wanting.

One may now wonder how Christianity can be effective, if the commands are impossible to satisfy. But that for Tolstoy is precisely what can make it effective. The real Christian is one who does not deny that Christ's commands are good just because he cannot satisfy them. Rather he believes with his whole heart that they are good, that he cannot satisfy them and that therefore he is a sinner. That is purity of heart, so far as human beings are capable of it. It is exemplified in the parable of the Publican and the Pharisee. Both are praying in the temple. The Pharisee thanks God that he is not as other men. The Publican, by contrast, begs God to have mercy on him, a sinner. 'I tell you,' said Christ, 'it was this man who went home justified.'

These points are explained by Tolstoy with marvellous clarity in his Postface to *The Kreutzer Sonata*.[8] He says that there are two kinds of guidance. The first kind consists of commands, relative to human capacity, which people can fulfil, if they make an effort: for example, give up alcohol, fast on Fridays, and so on. He likens this kind to a fixed lamp, casting light on the ground immediately beneath it. Christ's commands are not of this kind. Tolstoy likens them to a lamp held in front of one as one walks. With every move, the lamp moves further ahead so that one cannot reach it. But the light it casts on the ground, as it moves, forms a path along which one can proceed. Similarly, Christ's commands, though they cannot be fulfilled in this life, will guide one forward if one aspires towards them.

Now Tolstoy's charge against the Christians of his time is that they have degraded Christ's commands to those of the first kind. On seeing that they cannot fulfil Christ's commands, they have not affirmed that nevertheless they should fulfil them, that they are sinners but, in order to justify themselves, have substituted others which they *can* fulfil. He illustrates the process by means of an analogy:

> 'Man is weak, he must be set a task that is within his power', people say. This is just the same as saying: 'My hands are weak, I cannot draw a line that is straight, the shortest one between two points, that is, and so, in order to make it easier for myself, instead of drawing the straight line I should like to draw, I shall take as my model a crooked or broken line.
> The weaker my hand is, the greater the need of a model that is perfect.'[9]

This is the process which is found, according to Tolstoy, in the Christian attitude to marriage. It is denied that Christ commanded chastity, for that is impossible to fulfil. What is possible is to confine sexual relations to marriage. Consequently it is marriage that is truly Christian.

Tolstoy's view is not, let it be noted, that marriage is bad. In relative terms, it may be good. His point is that in itself it has nothing to do with Christianity. The Christian ideal is not marriage, but celibacy. He claimed, moreover, that once Christians sacrificed the ideal of celibacy they would sacrifice also the relative good of marriage. Thus he predicted, with remarkable prescience, that marriage and the family would prove more deeply rooted amongst Muslims and Jews than amongst Christians.[10] His argument was that the corruption of the best produces the worst. The Christians have the highest ideal but once the ideal is shifted from celibacy to marriage, it will be shifted from marriage to something else. Thus, so the argument might run, it is not possible to confine sexual relations to marriage. What is possible is to confine these to a free, loving relationship. Consequently it is a free loving sexual relationship which is truly Christian.[11]

A similar point is illustrated in *Hadji Murat*, Tolstoy's last story and one of his greatest achievements. The story has proved a puzzle to his commentators. It is commonly claimed, for example, that its theme is in conflict with Tolstoy's own views. At the time when he wrote the story, Tolstoy professed non-violence. But the main character in the story, and the most admirable, is a Muslim warrior who dies fighting, with great courage. A common explanation is that Tolstoy's artistic instincts overcame his religious views and that he wrote the story as a personal indulgence. But this interpretation is quite illusory. It has its source in the fallacious assumption that Tolstoy forsook art for simple moralizing. Thus it is true that Hadji Murat is a warrior and that we admire the courage with which he fights to the death. But he is not a Christian. His admirable qualities show themselves, most strikingly, by contrast with the Russians who frequent court circles, to whom he is introduced when he switches to the Russian side. The Russians, who are Christians, profess an ideal which is superior to that of Hadji Murat. But there is another difference between them. They are false to their ideal whilst he is true to his. In short, the false Christian is not better but worse than the true Muslim. In no respect does the story conflict with Tolstoy's later views. Quite the contrary, it exemplifies them.

The great misery of Tolstoy's last years was that his wife was unable to follow him in his views. She thought, like so many of his critics, that he had sacrificed his talent and, in addition, had endangered the welfare of his family. It is not necessary for us to consider the details of this relationship, which was at its worst during the last ten years of his life. We are concerned with Tolstoy's life only so far as it forms a background to his views on art. In any case the reader will find sufficient detail in the biographies. Troyat, for example, spends more than one hundred pages on the last ten years of Tolstoy's life, revealing the intimate details of the relationship. It is fair to warn the reader, however, that the biographers of Tolstoy tend to follow the approach of those, early in the century, who were concerned to debunk the Victorians. The guiding idea behind their writings, roughly speaking, is that greatness will not survive close scrutiny. Consequently close scrutiny is applied in order to detect every vice, folly and inconsistency in their subjects. Tolstoy is especially liable to this treatment since he professed religious views and is therefore suspected of thinking himself better than other people. It is not necessary to reply to these charges, for the reply has already been given by Tolstoy himself:

> 'Well, but you, Leo Nikolayevich; you preach, but how about practice?' People always put it to me and always triumphantly shut my mouth with it. You preach, but how do you live? And I reply that I do not preach and cannot preach, though I passionately desire to do so. I could only preach deeds; and my deeds are bad. What I say is not a sermon, but only a refutation of a false understanding of the Christian teaching and an explanation of its real meaning ... The performance of Christ's five commandments gives that meaning. If you wish to be a Christian, you must fulfil those commands. If you do not wish to fulfil them, don't talk of Christianity ... I do not fulfil a ten-thousandth part it is true, and I am to blame for that; but it is not because I do not wish to fulfil them that I fail, but because I do not know how to. Teach me how to escape from the nets of temptation that have ensnared me, help me, and I will fulfil them; but even without help I desire and hope to do so. Blame me – I do that myself – but blame *me*, and not the path I tread, and show to those who ask me where in my opinion the road lies! If I know the road home and go along it drunk, staggering from side to side – does that make the road along which I go a wrong one?'[12]

## Notes

1. D. H. Lawrence, *Selected Critical Writings*, Oxford, OUP, 1998, p. 42. Some of Lawrence's criticisms of Tolstoy are answered by F. R. Leavis, in a fine essay on *Anna Karenina*. See F. R. Leavis, *Anna Karenina and Other Essays*, London, Chatto and Windus, 1967, pp. 9–32.
2. Henri Troyat, *Tolstoy*, London, W. H. Allen, 1968.
3. Maxim Gorky, *Tolstoy, Chekhov and Andreev*, Letchworth, The Hogarth Press, 1934, p. 61.
4. See Isaiah Berlin, *Russian Thinkers*, Harmondsworth, Penguin, 1978, pp. 24–8.
5. A. N. Wilson evaluates the work differently. It will be worth quoting him, if only to reveal the attitude adopted towards Tolstoy even by a sympathetic modern critic. 'Once one is alerted to the danger signals, *A Confession*, precisely because of its artless sincerity, is revealed as a transparent piece of self-deception: transparent that is to everyone except the author' (*Tolstoy*, London, Hamish Hamilton, 1988, p. 312).

    Artless sincerity and self-deception are supposed to be conflicting qualities. In Tolstoy they are miraculously combined so that he is prevented from detecting his self-deception by his very sincerity. In order to reveal Tolstoy's self-deception, Wilson resorts to a technique that has been wittily exposed by Aylmer Maude. It consists in making an exception to a statement which Tolstoy intended in the first place only as a generality. For example, should he say 'Everyone knows that $2 + 2 = 4$', the critic replies 'No. My six month old baby does not know it.' Thus Wilson objects to Tolstoy's statement that before his conversion he led a sensual and worldly life by claiming that in his boyhood he flirted with Orthodoxy.

    It is worth noting that Tolstoy, in Wilson's view, exhausted his talent in writing *Anna Karenina*. The evidence for this is that after *Anna Karenina*, Tolstoy concentrated on the shorter literary forms. Now there have been great writers who concentrated almost exclusively on the shorter literary forms. Chekhov is an example. This has not prevented their being treated as masters. To go on and excel in the short form, having excelled in the long, is a supreme achievement. In Tolstoy it is treated as an artistic failure.

    We may note, finally, that there is no mystery about why Tolstoy switched to shorter forms. He wished to write in a form more accessible to ordinary people and, also, to deal directly with religious and social problems. None of this would have been possible had he concentrated on writing novels as long as *War and Peace* or even *Anna Karenina*. The latter took him four years to write; the former, six.
6. I have here transposed two sentences by Hugh Kingsmill. 'The mind is not an originating organ, and when it spins systems of thought out of itself, the results are valueless. Its function is to formulate what the whole being of man, will, heart and spirit, has experienced' (*D. H. Lawrence*, London, Methuen, 1938, p. 64).
7. See *What I Believe*, London, The Free Age Press, 1884, pp. 66–100.
8. See *The Kreutzer Sonata and Other Stories*, Harmondsworth, Penguin, 1985, pp. 267–83.
9. Ibid, p. 281.
10. Ibid., p. 276.
11. It is worth noting that D. H. Lawrence, in his story *The Man Who Died*, advocated precisely that view. Moreover, in the trial which arose over the publication of *Lady Chatterley's Lover*, his views were defended by some leading churchmen.
12. Quoted by A. N. Wilson in *How Can We Know?*, Harmondsworth, Penguin, 1985. Wilson's treatment of Tolstoy in his long biography seems to me inferior to his treatment in this shorter work.

CHAPTER TWO

# Art and Society

Tolstoy is concerned in *What is Art?* with certain tendencies in the arts of his time. These tendencies have their source in the so-called Romantic period. It will be useful to consider for a moment how they arose.

The term 'Romantic' is vague, having a number of uses. But its primary reference to the arts is historical. It picks out the artists who were at work in Europe during the first part of the nineteenth century. It implies, also, that those artists resembled one another in ways that distinguished them from their predecessors in the eighteenth century. In a number of the arts, for example, there was a reaction against earlier forms. Thus in poetry Wordsworth and Coleridge objected to the stereotyped language of the eighteenth century, its use of certain words as intrinsically poetical, and introduced the language of common speech. In music, there was a movement towards more fluent forms. The eighteenth-century symphony or sonata had the structure of exposition, sometimes repeated, development, recapitulation and coda. In this form, blocks of material have to be repeated. Composers such as Berlioz and Liszt eliminated these repetitions, producing music which approached continuous development, the unity of the music being preserved by the use in a work or movement of the same themes. There appeared also an element of personal feeling, in Beethoven, for example, which had been present in earlier composers, such as Mozart, but which now became more insistent. In painting, artists began to take their subjects from ordinary life rather than from the Bible or from classical mythology. The vague outline was sometimes preferred to the clear, especially in the interest of colour. These changes within the arts had causes which were not immediately artistic. To some extent, they were responses to changes in society more generally. For example, there were significant changes in the role of the artist. In the eighteenth century the artist had a role not significantly different from that of the craftsman. A painter, for example, acquired his art by being apprenticed to an established practitioner. Having acquired his art, he would look around for his own customers. The arts, in short, were taken to exist for the same reason that the crafts existed. There were needs to be supplied and the artist, like the craftsman, supplied them. Thus people had horses and needed them shod. The blacksmith existed to supply that need. He did not think of his skill as something he had created. He had learned it from other blacksmiths who were passing on what they themselves had acquired. People also needed music, in religious services, weddings, funerals, dances; churches needed representations of Christ and the Saints; princes and public figures wanted representations of themselves in paint or stone; there was a need for houses, temples, palaces. The musician, painter, sculptor, architect existed to supply those needs. In other words, the artist, like the craftsman, existed because he performed a social function.

Now the role of the artist began to change during the Romantic period. By the end of the nineteenth century it had been completely transformed. The artist was now to be understood precisely by contrast with the craftsman. The craftsman employs a set technique to achieve predetermined ends. What he seeks to produce can be specified in detail beforehand and if he does his job well he will produce only what any other craftsman would have produced who did the job equally well. By contrast, the artist is essentially creative and original. Thus the poet does not seek to reproduce what other poets produce, however good. His aim is to produce something new. For that reason, you cannot specify beforehand what he is going to produce; it is he who creates it. He caters, therefore, to no pre-existing demand. Rather he expresses his own thoughts and feelings, his personal vision.

As we have said, this change in the role of the artist has its source in the Romantic period. What are its causes? Like any other social phenomenon, its causes are various and here we can only indicate some of the most important. One of these is the French Revolution, an event of enormous significance in the history of Europe. The event seemed unprecedented. A whole society had been transformed, not as the result of some natural disaster but of deliberate intent, through the creative power of the human will. A new society was promised which would answer more nearly to human aspirations. The arts could no longer have the place they had in the old society, for that society no longer existed. New forms were needed and, in developing those forms, the artist would be in the forefront in creating a new kind of society. Marx, in his early writings, likened the relations between people in a free society to those that hold amongst a community of artists. A story often told about Beethoven illustrates the new attitude. Once when he and Goethe were walking together, they met members of the local aristocracy. Goethe stopped and bowed. Beethoven walked on. Then he turned to Goethe and said, 'We should not bow to them. They should bow to us.' The story is perhaps apocryphal, but the attitude was real enough. Artists, in short, no longer saw themselves as occupying a subordinate position to those representatives of the old order. They were heralds of a new and better order and were therefore superior to those representatives.

The French Revolution did not fulfil the hopes of its supporters. It was commerce rather than art which proved the dominant force during the nineteenth century, this being one of the high-points of the Industrial Revolution. The effect was to alienate artists from their society rather than to integrate them within it. The key to industrial success lay in the mass production of cheap goods. Some of these products served to replace the artist. An obvious example was photography. In the eighteenth century if you wanted the likeness of any person, you had no choice but to hire an artist. In the nineteenth, you could hire a photographer. To the layman, the photograph seemed the better likeness; it was also quicker to produce and much cheaper. But the whole industrial process seemed alien to art. It flourished through the use of machines rather than through individual skills, laboriously acquired. It aimed not at finished workmanship but at immediate profit, this being achieved by catering to the most insistent desires amongst the greatest number of people.

The effect of this development was to produce a distinction between two kinds of art. There was, on the one hand, low, popular or commercial art and, on the other, high or sophisticated art. It is necessary, however, to consider this distinction carefully, because it superficially resembles a different distinction. In European culture, there had always been a difference between popular and sophisticated art. But this is not the difference that developed towards the end of the nineteenth century. The important point is that the earlier difference between popular and sophisticated art is a matter of degree. You might even say that the latter is a development of the former, so that there is no sharp break between the two. For example, the songs of Schubert are evidently sophisticated but they have clear connections with folk songs, the songs of the people. Indeed, there is an occasional song where it would be hard to say whether it is a folk song or the work of a sophisticated artist. The same is true of instrumental music. Symphonic music, the most complicated form of instrumental music, developed among the Germans. But the Germans had an instrumental culture. The playing of instruments was a common pastime, families gathering to play for their own entertainment, so that the more complicated forms of instrumental music had their roots in a common culture. The same applies to other forms of art which flourished in the earlier part of the nineteenth century. The two most important were opera and the novel. Both these art forms had a wide public. Dickens, for example, was at once a popular and a sophisticated artist. Again, opera flourished in Italy, where it was a common form of entertainment, attended by all classes of people.

In the earlier part of the nineteenth century, therefore, there was still no sharp distinction between popular and sophisticated art. But it was just such a distinction that arose towards the end of that century. Thus the distinction between high and low art is one of kind rather than degree. Those who practise high art look down on low art as cheap or debased. Those who enjoy low art find high art largely unintelligible. Hence we find the sophisticated artists losing contact with a wide audience and disdaining the art that has popular appeal. They are content to produce their work for a select audience, consisting often enough entirely of their fellow artists. The effect of this, of course, was to make their work even more unintelligible to a wider audience.

It was in these circumstances that the sophisticated artist embraced the doctrine of art for art's sake. The doctrine was formulated in the 1830s by Théophile Gautier in his famous preface to *Mademoiselle de Maupin*:

> No, imbeciles! No! Fools and cretins that you are, a book will not make a plate of soup; a novel is not a pair of boots; a sonnet is not a syringe; a drama is not a railway ... No, two hundred thousand times, no.[1]

For Gautier, art is not an industrial product, justified by its social utility. Nor yet does it cater to an audience, whether popular or select. Its aim is to produce beauty which, even if it is appreciated by the artist alone, is a sufficient end, whether in art or in life. On this view, the separation between artist and audience, to which we have referred, was not a misfortune. For the true artist does not aim at an audience. He is justified by the inherent worth of his art. Gautier's formulation was early.[2] The doctrine flourished in the closing decades of the nineteenth century, being given a witty formulation by Oscar Wilde. But it exerted a great influence, especially in the visual arts, throughout the succeeding century.

Some appreciation of the developments sketched above is essential in understanding *What is Art?* Tolstoy's view in this work is directly opposed to the one formulated by Gautier. He holds that art is essentially a form of communication, requiring an audience as well as an artist, art lying precisely in the relation between the two. He holds, further, that the sophisticated art of the late nineteenth century is not high or well developed but decadent. A symptom of its decadence is the very difference between high and low art. For Tolstoy, art cannot flourish where it is isolated from the wider activities of the society in which it occurs. Its very force, where it flourishes, depends on its having an expressive relation to those activities. Sometimes he states his view in an exaggerated and intemperate form. But even in this form his view cannot be understood without understanding also some of the developments sketched above. For example, he claims that genuine art can be appreciated by everyone. But Tolstoy's 'everyone' has certain tacit exceptions. He is not thinking, for example, of the urbanized worker, of whom he had little experience. Russia, in his time, had not been industrialized. He is thinking of the folk, the peasants – not those who are devoid of culture but those who have a culture of their own. We may illustrate the point by reference to Russian folk song. The *Volga Boat Song*, for example, was made famous by the great bass Chaliapin, in the 1900s. It originated among the boatmen who worked along the Volga. There is a wealth of these songs, originating among the people, many of them recorded by the great Russian singers.[3] They were exploited also by the instrumental composers. Stravinsky begins *The Rite of Spring* by echoing one of them. Indeed, we may affirm, at least as a rough generalization, that we are hearing a folk song whenever, in sophisticated modern music, we hear real melodic inspiration. Thus the culture of the Russian people, in Tolstoy's time, was not supplied through various media, based in a metropolitan centre, or in a quite different country, by artists whose lives had nothing in common with those of their audience. The people had their own songs, dances, stories and ceremonies, sometimes of matchless quality. What Tolstoy is asserting, though in an intemperate way, is that in a flourishing culture the sophisticated arts will be an outgrowth from the popular, so that there will be a unity in the arts between their popular and sophisticated forms. A situation in which the art of the people is despised by the sophisticated and the art of the sophisticated unintelligible to the people is precisely one of decadence.

But to see these points in more detail, let us turn to Tolstoy's book.

**Notes**

1 Quoted in I. Berlin, *The Roots of Romanticism*, London, Chatto and Windus, 1999, p. 13.
2 As we shall see later, it contains elements of another theory, often termed the romantic.
3 Russian singing makes an interesting study. At the operatic level, it was influenced by the Italian style, but even there it retains a strong native element, especially evident in its great basses.

CHAPTER THREE

# The Problem

Tolstoy begins *What is Art?* by emphasizing the cost and labour involved in artistic activity. Throughout Europe, he says, thousands of people are occupied in writing, composing and painting. Moreover, in addition to the labour of artists themselves, there is the labour of thousands of others. A single opera performance, for example, requires not simply singers and orchestral players but an army of people to make costumes, arrange the scenery, clean the building, and so on. To illustrate these points, Tolstoy describes a visit he made to the rehearsal for a new opera. He describes how he entered the theatre through a side entrance, passed the people at work behind the scenes, the dozens of extras, and arrived in the main part of the theatre where the rehearsal was already in progress, under the direction of the dancing master, the dramatic coach and the conductor. The object of their attentions was a procession of Indians. In describing what he then saw, Tolstoy uses one of his favourite devices:

> The procession is preceded by a recitative, delivered by a man dressed up like some variety of Turk, who opening his mouth in a curious way, sings, 'Home I bring the bri-i-de'. He sings and waves his arm (which is of course bare) from under his mantle. The procession commences.

But it was immediately stopped. The French Horn had played a wrong note and was abused – 'as cabmen abuse one another' – by the conductor. The procession recommenced:

> The Indians with their halberds again come on, treading softly in their extraordinary boots; again the singer sings 'Home I bring the bri-i-de'. But here the pairs get too close together. More raps with the stick, more scolding, and a recommencement. Again 'Home I bring the bri-i-de', again the same gesticulation with the bare arm from under the mantle, and again the couples, treading softly with halberds on their shoulders, some with sad and serious faces, some talking and smiling, arrange themselves in a circle and begin to sing.[1]

The device that Tolstoy uses in the above passages is sometimes called the alienation effect. We grasp a phenomenon, even in the simplest perception, through a hierarchy of details, some subordinate to others in their importance. Someone who is unfamiliar with the phenomenon does not know how to order its details and will therefore describe them indiscriminately. Tolstoy often describes a phenomenon in this way. In the present case, for example, he tells us that a man who sings opens his mouth in a curious way and that the words he produces are distorted when compared with ordinary speech. He mentions other details we are inclined to overlook, such as the work behind the scenes, the tedious labour of rehearsal, the loss of temper and so on. In short, he describes a phenomenon with which he is perfectly familiar as though it were an alien practice which he is viewing for the first time. As we shall see, this device has its dangers as well as its uses. But Tolstoy's aim in using it is to shock us into standing outside a practice, so that we might assess it as a whole and not simply in terms of its own conventions.

Now the cost and labour involved in artistic activity have been established. What has not been established is its function. Given the cost and labour involved, one would expect the function of art to be obvious and important. Tolstoy's next move is to deny that its function is at all obvious. For example, a performance such as he has described can bring little benefit to the majority of people, since they would find it largely unintelligible. He implies, indeed, that to most people the performance he has described would appear just as he has described it – as an alien practice which they can view only from the outside. But the situation is little better when one turns to artists themselves. For what one finds is not an agreement about the function of their activity but, on the contrary, a continual disagreement. In each branch of art, one finds different schools; the members of any given school reject the views expressed by members of all the others:

> The artists of various sects, like the theologians of various sects, mutually exclude and destroy one another. Listen to the artists of the schools of our times, and in all branches you will find each set of artists disowning others. In poetry the old romanticists deny the parnassians and the decadents; the parnassians disown the romanticists and the decadents; the decadents disown all their predecessors and the symbolists; the symbolists disown all their predecessors and *les mages*; and *les mages* disown all, all their predecessors. Among novelists we have naturalists, psychologists, and 'nature-ists', all rejecting each other. And it is the same in dramatic art, in painting, and in music.[2]

Tolstoy's references in the above passage are mainly to the poetic schools which flourished in France during the late nineteenth century. But it is unnecessary to distinguish among them, for the point intended is a general one. Confusion about the point or function of art is widespread not simply among the general public but among artists themselves. The main point of Tolstoy's book is now raised. Given the cost and labour involved, artistic activity seems to need justification. But the justification is not easy to find. The point of the book is to find it.

Tolstoy turns for assistance in his second chapter to the philosophers, to those who have occupied themselves with aesthetic questions. Among these, the distinguishing mark of artistic activity is said to be beauty. That was the view, it will be remembered, of Théophile Gautier. Beauty is that inner worth which distinguishes certain works of art and justifies the artistic activities. But this answer is not as satisfactory as at first it may appear. On reflection, for example, we may find the term 'beautiful' more appropriate to some works of aesthetic merit than to others. Thus it seems more appropriate to a lyric by Burns than to a tragedy by Shakespeare, such as *King Lear*. But *King Lear* is not inferior to a lyric by Burns; it is greater. In short, the beautiful seems not to be commensurate with aesthetic merit, there are great works which fall outside the category. Further, there are objects which fall inside the category but are not works of art. A sunset is not a work of art but may be very beautiful. There are further problems. Suppose we confine ourselves to beautiful objects. They form a bewildering variety. What, for example, is there in common between the beauty of a song, a sunset and a face? Someone who is puzzled about the nature of art, when told that it produces beauty, is likely to be equally puzzled about the nature of beauty.

Thus so far as the term beauty has a clear use, it applies to objects other than the artistic, and so far as it applies to artistic objects, it does not apply to them all. Tolstoy says that the point is especially evident to those who are confined to the Russian language. For in that language the term is clearly restricted in its use: it is applied only to objects that are pleasing to the sight. In Russian, according to Tolstoy, it would not be natural to describe a poem or a song as beautiful. Those confined to Russian, therefore, would find it especially implausible to define the whole of art in terms of it.

To confirm that beauty is inadequate in defining art, Tolstoy proceeds in his third chapter to a survey of aesthetics. It is not the happiest chapter in his book. In preparation for *What is Art?*, Tolstoy had read widely and he evidently wished to leave a record of his labours. Consequently in a single chapter he gives a history of aesthetics covering the preceding two hundred years. But the move was not a wise one. Great figures have to be covered in a few paragraphs, sometimes in a sentence or two, and the impression conveyed is inevitably one of superficiality or even unfairness.

Nevertheless some useful points emerge in Tolstoy's fourth chapter, where he assesses the philosophers he has surveyed. He divides them into two classes. Philosophers in the Continental tradition fall into one class; those in the English tradition into the other. Philosophers in both classes define art in terms of beauty, but whereas those in the Continental tradition treat beauty as an objective spiritual quality acquired by intuition, those in the English tradition treat it as a subjective quality relative to the observer. For the English, beauty reduces to pleasure, though it is pleasure of a special kind; for example, it is not based on self-interest. Tolstoy states that it is the English who give the better analysis of beauty. Roughly speaking, to affirm that an object is beautiful is to affirm that it affords a certain kind of pleasure. But just for that reason it is useless in distinguishing what is important in art. Tolstoy argues, in short, that the philosophers in both classes, the English no less than the Continental, were mistaken at the start in seeking to define art in terms of beauty. For since beauty is a subjective quality, it cannot supply what we need in understanding art.

Precisely the qualities we need are objective ones. Tolstoy explains himself by giving an analogy with food. Suppose we are told that people eat what pleases them. Even if this were true, it would tell us nothing of importance about food. A serious concern with food would concentrate not on subjective reactions but on the objective process of nourishment. Which food genuinely nourishes and which, though it may be pleasant, is harmful to the body? Now, similarly, those with a serious interest in art will not deny that some works please and others do not. But it is not what they wish to know. What concerns them is the objective process of art. What are its causes and consequences? What is its role in human life? How does it work for human good and how for evil? Those are the questions evaded in Classical aesthetics; yet they are the only important ones.

Tolstoy's attitude in dismissing some two hundred years of aesthetics may seem arrogant. In fact, however, many philosophers in more recent times have adopted the same attitude. In this they have been influenced by the philosophy of Wittgenstein, and it will be useful to consider his views for a moment, for they shed light on *What is Art?* Wittgenstein's influence is indirect. In his *Philosophical Investigations*, he argues that in our use of words we are not determined, as he formerly thought, by fixed boundaries.[3] He takes as an example the word 'game'. At first one may suppose that the meaning of 'game' must lie in some features common to its instances, for it is by virtue of these features that they all count as games. In fact, however, it is difficult to find common features. One can find features common to many. For example, many games are competitive, governed by rules and enjoyed for their own sakes. But these features appear among non-games. Moreover, there are games which lack them. Patience or solitaire is not competitive; ring a ring o' roses is not obviously governed by rules; professional football is not played simply for enjoyment.

At this point a thought may strike us. Even if game can be defined by reference to common features, its meaning cannot depend on our having the definition explicit in our minds. Although we do not have it explicit in our minds, we certainly know the meaning of the word game. It may then occur to us that meaning is a matter of practice rather than of theoretical definition. Where definitions occur they summarize what for the most part is acquired in other ways. Thus, for the most part, a word is defined when it *already* has a use, *already* has a meaning. Further reflection will reveal that in most cases definitions are unnecessary. That is because to define a word is to fix it, to determine for all time what will count as one of its instances. But there is a good reason why for the most part we should not want our words fixed in that way. Life is not fixed; we cannot anticipate everything we shall go on to experience. For example, we cannot anticipate what new games will arise in the distant future.

This does not mean, of course, that there are no relations between games, so that just anything may count as such. Wittgenstein likens the relations between games to resemblances in a family. Looking at a group photograph, you may suddenly notice that the group forms a family. You see the family face. But what does that mean? It certainly does not mean that there is one face common to the group, so that each member is an exact replica of the next. Rather, there are various features which keep appearing. Shape of chin or nose, colour of hair, general build, and so on – each of these can be seen as the same in various members of the group. There is a similarity in the resemblances between games. If we take certain cases as central, we may trace resemblances between them and others. But the others will not resemble them all in the same way. This game and that one will resemble the central cases in different ways, so that there will be no single set of resemblances which run through all games.

Wittgenstein's analysis has been criticized. Probably the most lucid criticism is by Maurice Mandelbaum.[4] He has two points. The first is that Wittgenstein's analysis allows no way of distinguishing games from other activities. The concept of a game cannot rest on resemblances between its instances since those resemblances extend to activities that are not games. For example, war is not a game. But there are resemblances between warfare and some central instances of a game. Thus warfare involves competing sides and usually, as in a game, one wins and the other loses. Indeed one can find some resemblance between any two things, so that if resemblances alone were the basis of a concept such as game, there would be no end to it. His second point is that a family resemblance is defined as holding amongst a family. Family itself is determined not by resemblance but by genetic kinship. Consequently there is in fact a common element among family resemblances. They are united by the genetic kinship which holds among members of a family. Similarly, he suggests, there may be a common basis to games, even if this does not appear on the surface.

These criticisms, though often expressed, are not as impressive as at first they may appear. For example, it is true that there are resemblances between games and other activities. It does not follow that those resemblances are more important than the differences. Thus, whatever the resemblances between war and certain games, there is the obvious difference that in war people are out to kill one another. To most people, that difference seems evidently more significant than any resemblance. That is why they would not call war a game. On examination, the second point also seems weak. Let us grant that the resemblances in a family have a common basis in genetics. It seems obvious that you do not need to know this in order to detect the resemblances. Indeed, you may detect the resemblances in a family through looking at a photograph, without knowing beforehand that it is a photograph of that family. You may come to this conclusion only *after* you have detected the resemblances. It seems obvious, also, that Wittgenstein mentions family resemblance in order to illustrate, not to define, the type of resemblance that interests him. It is the type of resemblance that often crops up in families. But genetic kinship is not essential to the type of relationship itself. Indeed, were that so, the example would be pointless, for Wittgenstein's whole aim in using it is to illustrate how the instances of a game are related to one another. But those instances are evidently not related by genetic kinship.

Granting, then, the validity of Wittgenstein's analysis, what is its relevance to aesthetics? The relevance will be evident if we return to the philosophers described by Tolstoy. They seem plainly to have assumed that in order to understand art, one must first define the word. They have assumed, further, that to define the word one must specify certain features common to all the arts. They have seized on beauty as the most likely candidate and have proceeded to define art in terms of it. But as many philosophers in more recent times have pointed out, the procedure is erroneous, for art, like game, stands for a family of cases, related by various resemblances and not by a single set. To understand art, therefore, we must proceed not by defining the word but by giving examples of the activities. Other examples will need to be given, as the occasion arises, but these can be readily supplied once we have a grasp on the central cases. The procedure is liberating rather than constricting. The frustrating feature of the traditional method is that we are perpetually returning to our starting-point. Having specified a definition, we find exceptions. We then have to scrap that definition and begin once more. But when we begin by giving examples, we know they are not exhaustive. As the need arises, we may supplement or qualify. But since we were not attempting, in the first place, to capture the whole of art in a few sentences, we are not forced with every qualification to scrap what we have achieved and begin all over again.

Now this in effect is Tolstoy's procedure. He defines art not by defining the word but by indicating what he calls objective qualities. In short, he indicates central features in artistic activities and traces their role in human life. Critics often misrepresent him through not grasping this procedure. They interpret his account on the basis of what he has said at this or that point in *What is Art?* They then criticize him by stating exceptions. Had they waited, they would frequently have found that Tolstoy, at a later point, has stated the exceptions himself. These points will become evident as we turn to the positive side of his account.

## Notes

1  *What is Art?*, London, The World Classics, 1955, p. 76.
2  Ibid., pp. 79–80.
3  L. Wittgenstein, *Philosophical Investigations*, Oxford, Blackwell, 1976, sections 65–8, pp. 31–2.
4  See M. Mandelbaum, *American Philosophical Quarterly*, vol. 2, 1965, pp. 218–28.

CHAPTER FOUR

# The Central Features

So far, Tolstoy has raised his main question and criticized responses to it he thinks mistaken. His approach has been mainly negative. In his fifth chapter, he begins his positive account by stating that art involves a relationship between the person who produces a work of art and those who receive it:

> Every work of art causes the receiver to enter into a certain kind of relationship both with him who produced or is producing the art, and with all those who, simultaneously, previously, or subsequently, receive the same artistic impression.[1]

In short, art is a form of communication. But we must be clear about the type of communication involved. If in ordinary speech I tell you how I feel, that is not art. But suppose I express my feelings through word or gesture in such a way that you in some manner come to share them. Now we are approaching nearer to art. To illuminate this point, Tolstoy refers to a phenomenon common in ordinary life. If one person laughs, another feels merry; or if a person weeps, another becomes sad. One is excited or irritated and others are brought to a similar state of mind. It is as though our feelings spread by *infection*. Feelings have, as it were, their natural signs or expressions; others through these signs or expressions are infected by our feelings. But here, still, we have only the roots of art, rather than art itself. For the infection involved is unconscious, automatic. We arrive at art through a *sophisticated development* of that process. Instead of natural signs, such as weeping or laughter, occurring unconsciously, we find conscious signs, such as words or pictures, used quite intentionally to produce a similar result. So art is the process by which one person gives conscious expression to what he feels in order to infect others with the same feeling. It follows, of course, that we become infected only by consciously attending to that expression. For art, though it has its roots in unconscious processes, involves the transformation of those processes through conscious signs or symbols. Tolstoy gives an example to illustrate these points:

> To take the simplest example: a boy having experienced, let us say, fear on encountering a wolf, relates that encounter, and in order to evoke in others the feeling he has experienced, he describes himself, his condition before the encounter, the surroundings, the wood, his own lightheartedness, and then the wolf's appearance, its movements, the distance between himself and the wolf, and so forth. All this, if only the boy when telling the story again experiences the feelings he had lived through, and infects the hearers and compels them to feel what he had experienced – is art.

Note that we are here being given an example, not an exhaustive definition. The caution is necessary, since some critics treat it as exhaustive. For example, the boy in Tolstoy's example is expressing an incident he has himself lived through. Robert Wilkinson, in a recent work, treats Tolstoy as stating a necessary condition for all art. Thus he says that for Tolstoy 'in any art worthy of the name, the artist must have lived through the feelings she or he wishes to express'.[2] He then criticizes Tolstoy's account on that basis. In short, he treats the example as though it were intended to provide a definition for art and does not wait to see whether Tolstoy, as the need arises, might supplement or qualify it. He would not have had to wait long. For Tolstoy qualifies it in the next sentence:

> Even if the boy had not seen a wolf but had frequently been afraid of one, and if wishing to evoke in others the fear he had felt, he invented an encounter with a wolf and recounted it so as to make his hearers share the feelings he experienced when he feared the wolf, that also would be art. And just in the same way it is art if a man, having experienced either the fear of suffering or the attraction of enjoyment (whether in reality or in imagination) expresses these feelings on canvas or in marble so that others are infected by them.[3]

As I implied in the last chapter, we should not expect Tolstoy to give us a water-tight definition of art. As we have seen, that is in any case impossible. What we need is a grasp on some features of art which are of central importance. For that purpose, the simpler or more primitive the example, the better it will be. We should know very well that art is a complicated business and that, later, we shall have to attend to other features. But we need something to hold on to. We need some thread to guide us through the labyrinth.

Now Tolstoy performs that task very well. Let us return to his example and alter it slightly. Suppose there were two boys who encountered the wolf. One gets back before the other. He is obviously upset; we gather he has encountered a wolf; but otherwise we get nothing very coherent out of him. Then the second boy returns. Not only does he relate what occurred but he brings it vividly before us, so that it is as if we see the wolf and, for a moment, share the boys' fear. Now one thing is certain. That boy is a born story-teller. He has in him some of the essentials of an artist. In short, we have here a simple example of a genuine artistic experience. At this stage, that is all we need. We have something to hold on to.

We need now to reflect on what we have. The example gives us some of the central features in art. What then are those features? We note, first, that the second boy did not simply tell us *that* something had happened. The other boy did that. But the second boy in some sense recreated what happened. It was as if we were seeing it for ourselves, were experiencing it as he did. That is what Tolstoy calls infection. At this stage, we need not analyse the phenomenon; we need only to recognize its reality. There is a parallel phenomenon in the case of memory. Sometimes we just remember that something has occurred. But sometimes the past seems to return to us. Once again – or so it seems – we experience what occurred many years ago. Now the genuine artist is one who can in that way recreate for us events we have never experienced at all.

That then, for Tolstoy, is one central feature of genuine art. But there is another. So far as the artist recreates for us what we have not experienced, he thereby enlarges our experience. Moreover, in enlarging our experience, he gives us a better understanding of people hitherto unknown to us. For example, the first boy cannot express himself. We are at a distance from him. The second can express his experience and we are no longer at a distance. We now share the experience not simply of the second boy *but also of the first*. Through his art, the second boy has brought us all together.

So far as art brings us together, it fulfils a function. Perhaps it would be better to say 'role', for 'function' can be misleading. We naturally associate the word with a functional object, such as a fire-extinguisher. The fire-extinguisher is constructed to fulfil a conscious purpose. The 'function' of art is not in that way consciously contrived. Moreover, a work of art interests us in itself and not simply so far as it fulfils a purpose. Thus we begin to tell a child a story. 'Once upon a time,' we say, 'in the country of Alfania, a prince who had been travelling for many days arrived at an ancient castle.' If the child is in the mood, he starts thinking: Who is the prince? Why is he travelling? When he gets to the castle, what is going to happen to him? In short, the child is already interested. He needs no reason or inducement to become so. The story has drawn him into itself. Nevertheless it is as though nature had a purpose in so drawing him. Tolstoy here makes a comparison with speech. Through speech, a child without knowing it is drawn into human life and becomes fully human. Similarly, through art, he enlarges his understanding of that human life into which he has been drawn. The function is natural, not contrived. In other words, in listening to a story we are interested in the story itself rather than in understanding life. Nevertheless we increase our understanding of life through our interest in the story. Thus art has a vital function or role in human life:

> As every man, thanks to man's capacity to express thoughts by words, may know all that has been done for him in the realms of thought by all humanity before his day, and can in the present, thanks to his capacity to understand the thought of others, become a sharer in their activity and also himself hand on to his contemporaries and descendants the thoughts he has assimilated from others as well as those that have arisen in himself; so, thanks to man's capacity to be infected with the feelings of others by means of art, all that is being lived through by his contemporaries is accessible to him, as well as the feelings experienced by men thousands of years ago, and he has also the possibility of transmitting his own feelings to others.
>
> If people lacked the capacity to receive the thoughts conceived by men who preceded them and to pass on to others their own thoughts, men would be like wild beasts ...

> And if men lacked this other capacity of being infected by art, people might be almost more savage still, and above all more separated from, and more hostile to, one another.
> And therefore the activity of art is a most important one, as important as the activity of speech itself and as generally diffused.[4]

The point is the more evident when we realize that sophisticated art is only one aspect of artistic activities which run through society:

> We are accustomed to understand art to be only what we hear or see in theatres, concerts and exhibitions together with buildings, statues, poems and novels ... But all this is but the smallest part of the art by which we communicate with one another in life. All human life is filled with works of art of every kind – from cradle-song, jest, mimicry, the ornamentation of houses, dress and utensils, to church services, buildings, monuments and triumphal processions. It is all artistic activity.[5]

It may be noted that Tolstoy has now briefly sketched the ground, characteristics and role of artistic activities. They have their ground in natural or instinctive expressions of feeling. They have as one of their chief characteristics what he calls infection, the re-creation by the artist of experiences which his audience can share. They have a role in being 'a means of union among men joining them together in the same feelings, and being indispensable for the life and progress towards well-being of individuals and of humanity'.[6] All this Tolstoy has accomplished not by abstract definitions, but by turning to the activities themselves.

Yet, as we have said, there is always the need to supplement and to qualify. For example, Tolstoy has said that art is a means of unity among human beings. But that surely is not necessarily true. It can also be a means of disunity. For example, it can be used to stimulate hatred, to set one group of people against another. Tolstoy is well aware of the point. For example, towards the end of his fifth chapter, he refers to Plato's view of art. Plato was so alive to the dangers of art, its powers of corruption, that he considered circumstances in which it might be prohibited. Tolstoy disagrees with Plato but he treats his view with respect. He says it is preferable to the view that the aim of art is pleasure. For at least Plato recognizes that art is a serious business, having important consequences for human life.

To see how Tolstoy copes with Plato's point, we must move to the next stage in his account. He argues that if art is to perform its function for good, it must be evaluated in moral and not simply in aesthetic terms. Thus it is true that not all art unites. But not all art is good. Having become clear about the importance of art for life, we should use that knowledge in discriminating between works of art. For example, we should treat as bad those works which promote discord and hatred, and as good those works which promote harmony and well-being. Here we touch on the relation in Tolstoy's account between the moral and the aesthetic. It is complicated and I do not believe it is well understood. We must give it detailed treatment in our next chapter.

**Notes**

1   *What is Art?*, p. 120.
2   'Art, Emotion and Expression', in *Philosophical Aesthetics: An Introduction*, ed. O. Hanfling, Oxford, Blackwell, 1992, p. 186. For an excellent criticism of Wilkinson's interpretation see Todd R. Long, 'A Selective Defence of Tolstoy's *What is Art?*', *Philosophical Writings*, no. 8, Summer 1998, pp. 15–25.
3   *What is Art?*, p. 122.
4   Ibid., pp. 123–4.
5   Ibid., pp. 124–5.
6   Ibid., p. 123.

CHAPTER FIVE

# Art and Morality

As we have said, the next stage in Tolstoy's account involves his considering the relation in art between the moral and the aesthetic. It is important to emphasize that the moral does not enter at all into the earlier stages. The elements which Tolstoy there takes as indispensable to art are morally neutral. The power of infection, for example, which he takes as indispensable to genuine art, may work for good or ill. The point is important since, as we have seen, many critics assume that for Tolstoy it is the moral alone that gives value to art. Robert Wilkinson, for example, says that on Tolstoy's account:

> the subject matter of a work of art largely or wholly determines its aesthetic merit or demerit. That is, for anyone holding the Tolstoyan premise, it follows that the presence of whatever subject-matter is ideologically approved of guarantees success in a work of art, and its absence or contradiction guarantees indifference or failure.[1]

This passage can be challenged at a number of points. For example, it very strongly suggests that Tolstoy, or one of his consistent followers, can approve of art only if it expresses his own ideology. That is plainly false. Tolstoy's view is that genuine art expresses beliefs that go deep in its culture. The beliefs of that culture need not be his own. As we shall see, for example, he admired medieval art, though he rejected the Catholicism it expressed.

The more important point, however, is that Wilkinson misinterprets Tolstoy's view of the relation between morality and art. For Tolstoy art is not absolutely autonomous. It draws its force from beliefs and feelings not in themselves artistic. But it has a relative autonomy. Those beliefs and feelings have a value in art only when they are expressed in artistic terms. Todd Long makes this point in his perceptive criticism of Wilkinson.[2] As he says, Tolstoy takes infection as an indispensable element in the success of art. Indeed Tolstoy states, quite explicitly, that one may detect infectious power in a work, and therefore attribute it value without judging its moral content. '*The stronger the infection, the better is the art, as art*, speaking of it now apart from its subject matter – that is, not considering the value of the feelings it transmits.'[3]

There are many other passages where Tolstoy makes the same point, quite as explicitly. As Long says, it is impossible, on the basis of these passages, to suppose that the value of art, for Tolstoy, is determined solely by its moral content.

Nevertheless, I do not think Long's own interpretation is entirely accurate. On his view, Tolstoy distinguishes two types of evaluation, one involving aesthetic terms, the other moral. In aesthetic terms one judges whether a work is genuine or counterfeit art; in moral terms, whether it is good or bad. The aesthetic judgement deals with the *form* of the work, the moral with its *content*. Long acknowledges that Tolstoy does not confine himself to these categories. For example, he sometimes judges a work bad on aesthetic ground. But he treats this as an inconsistency on Tolstoy's part. I do not think this account is sound. Tolstoy's view, rather, is that in evaluating a work as good or bad, we make a *complex* judgement involving *both* moral and aesthetic elements, taking in *both* form and content. For him, the two can be separated, as different aspects, during a process of analysis. But they cannot be kept separate in a final evaluation, because the two are organically connected. Long, himself, quotes Tolstoy to this effect. Thus he quotes his speaking of 'the chief property of art – wholeness, organicness, in which form and content constitute an inseparable whole expressing the feeling experienced by the artist'.[4] In short, Tolstoy's account is subtler than even Long allows.

These points will be the more evident, if we reflect in some detail on the relation in art between form and content. A little reflection will reveal that the distinction is relative. What, for one purpose, is content may for another be form. For example, the form of a sonnet will be constituted by a certain rhyme scheme, a certain number of lines, and so on. Here we make no mention of the words, which count as content. Two sonnets will have the same form, though they use quite different words, say quite different things. But we can also distinguish between form and content, concentrating simply on the words. For example, two poems using quite different words may yield the same paraphrase: happiness is momentary, lasting but a day, so seize it as it arises. The words of the poems now count not as content but as form, being the style with which they express in their different ways the same paraphrasable content. In other contexts, we may shift the distinction yet again. For example, we may say that the real content of a poem is not its paraphrase but what it conveys in its total expression. Thus one poem in its total expression may convey to those who 'seize the day' an attitude of disparagement; another, an attitude of praise. Here the two poems, though they have the same paraphrase, will yield not simply different but opposing contents.

This shift between form and content is bewildering only in the abstract. In the concrete, it is usually clear, because we know what purpose is in view and therefore what counts as form and what as content. The shift itself arises through our moving among different aspects of a single whole. If we concentrate for the moment on what we call form, we are not denying the existence of other aspects, equally valid. The point is evident in our example of sonnet form. Here we exclude the words. But without the words there would be no sonnet and therefore no form. The words are excluded only in the sense that for the moment we do not give them our special attention. In a similar fashion, we may ignore the shape of an object in order to concentrate on its colour, though in fact no object can have a colour without having a shape. It is clear, therefore, that the distinction between form and content is relative to what aspects of a work we consider. We cannot consider some aspects without ignoring others. But since the aspects are organically related, the one we consider at the moment cannot be final. It may be useful in considering a work to make some distinction between form and content, treating the former as aesthetic and the latter as moral. Tolstoy's point is that in a final assessment of the work, as good or bad, they must be taken together.

In short, there is no such thing as the assessment of a work first as an aesthetic entity and then as a moral one, each assessment being independent of the other. There can be a partial assessment of the work as infectious, leaving aside for the moment other aspects. But the assessment is essentially partial. We cannot transfer what it suggests to the work as a whole. For what it suggests may well have to be modified when we consider the other aspects.

This interrelation between the aesthetic and the moral, or between form and content, is well illustrated by Tolstoy's own critical practice. We may take as an example his criticism of Maupassant's *Une Partie de Campagne*.[5] The story concerns two men who are out rowing and who meet and seduce two women, a mother and her daughter. Maupassant handles the incident in a light and amusing manner. Tolstoy says that the effect would have been different had he described the incident from both sides, the women's as well as the men's. In fact, the women's feelings are entirely excluded. It will be salutary to consider whether that criticism is moral or aesthetic. One will find that it can be expressed as easily in the one category as in the other. For example, one may say that Maupassant in his story gives expression to a false or distorted view of life. That would suggest the story was at fault in its moral content. But one could as easily say that in his *handling* of his story he falsified the incidents it describes. That would suggest the story is at fault in the *treatment* of its content and therefore in its aesthetic form. But the criticism is the same, however one puts it.

Tolstoy's essay on Maupassant may be taken as a demonstration of how in the best criticism it is impossible to divorce the moral from the aesthetic. It involves, for example, a brilliant and witty exposure of the sentimentality which runs through the type of realism that Maupassant practises at his worst:

> Accustomed as we are to read in French novels of how families live in threes, always with a lover known to everyone except the husband, it still remains quite unintelligible to us how it happens that all husbands are always fools, cocus et ridicules, but all lovers (who themselves in the end marry and become husbands) are not only not cocus et ridicules, but are heroic. And still less comprehensible is it how all women can be depraved, and yet all mothers saintly.[6]

Perhaps one should say 'inverted sentimentality'. The sentimentalist suppresses the nasty side of life in order to wallow in the nice; the realist, in Maupassant's sense, suppresses the nice in order to wallow in the nasty. As Tolstoy shows, the effect either way is bad, both in art and in life.

It should now be evident that Tolstoy, in his view of the relation between art and morality, is not committed to the extreme didacticism so often attributed to him. We may test the point by turning, for the last time, to Wilkinson's interpretation. As we have seen, he holds that for Tolstoy the value of a work is derived largely or wholly from its subject matter. If this interpretation is correct, it follows for Tolstoy that two works having the same subject matter are interchangeable. Since their only value is in what they have in common, we can substitute one for the other. Wilkinson takes this to be a decisive refutation of Tolstoy's view:

> To give one example: there are a number of pieces of music dating from roughly the turn of the century which are 'farewells to life', for example, the Ninth symphony of Bruckner and the Tenth of Mahler. If Tolstoy is right, it is unimportant if one of these works is lost, but to say this is to see at once that it is false. The reason for the falsehood lies in the fact that in each case the poignancy is embodied in a unique fashion and the uniqueness is constituted by the special combination of aesthetic properties employed in each case. Any theory of aesthetic expression must acknowledge that the vehicle of expression – the particular work of art itself – makes an ineliminable contribution to the expression.[7]

Now it is true that Bruckner's Ninth Symphony and Mahler's Tenth may be described as farewells to life. But that is to describe them in the manner of a paraphrase. As we have seen, two works which yield the same paraphrase may differ strikingly in their total content. For example, one farewell to life may be embittered, another resigned; a third may be defiant. Consequently even if the value of a work lay wholly in its content, it still would not follow that Bruckner's Ninth is interchangeable with Mahler's Tenth.

But what is most evidently false in the above passage is its assumption that for Tolstoy the details of a particular work are irrelevant to what it expresses. To refute this assumption, Todd Long has only to quote the following passage from *What is Art?*:

> A musical performance is art and can infect only when the sound is neither higher nor lower than it ought to be – that is, the infinitely small centre of the required note must be played – and it must have exactly the necessary duration, and the intensity of sound must be neither stronger nor weaker than is necessary. The least deviation in pitch of the sound one way or the other, the least lengthening or shortening of the duration, and the least strengthening or weakening of the sound as compared with what is required, destroys the perfection of the performance, and consequently the infectiousness of the work ... It is the same with all the arts: a little bit lighter, a little bit darker, a little bit higher, lower, to the right, to the left – in painting; a little bit weaker or stronger in intonation, a little bit too early or too late – in dramatic art: in poetry – a little bit too much said, or not

said, or exaggerated, and there is no infection. Infection is achieved only when and in so far as the artist finds those infinitely small moments of which the work of art is composed.[8]

We are now dealing, as we have said, with the second stage of Tolstoy's account. In the earlier stage, he had established that art is a form of communication, involving a kind of infection, by which the artist recreates for his audience the experiences of life. The infection is not automatic or unconscious. It depends on the use of conscious symbols, so that the infectious power of a work will depend on the ability of the artist to produce just those details which will infect his audience and the active attention of that audience to those details. Tolstoy now introduces the moral element. But it enters as the stuff of art, not as an alien material imposed from the outside. The stuff of art is human experience. Human experience is permeated with good and evil. Consequently, whether art fulfils its function for good in human life will depend on an active sense of good and evil in artists and their public. Tolstoy will soon consider how active is that sense in the art of his contemporaries. But first he provides a background, by considering the role of art in earlier societies. Here he takes a further step. He argues that art performs its function for good where the sense of good and evil is nourished by a religious conception of life.

**Notes**

1  Wilkinson, 'Art, Emotion and Expression', p. 184.
2  Long, 'A Selective Defence', p. 17.
3  *What is Art?*, p. 228.
4  Long, 'A Selective Defence', p. 24.
5  Included in the same volume as *What is Art?*, p. 22.
6  Ibid., p. 30.
7  Wilkinson, 'Art, Emotion and Expression', p. 185.
8  Long, 'A Selective Defence', p. 20.

CHAPTER SIX

# Art in History

We have already noted the dominance in the late nineteenth century of the view that art affords its own pleasure in the beauty of its objects. Tolstoy now proceeds to show that this is a late development. In earlier societies, he argues, art had its role in expressing what for that society constituted the meaning of life. The best art was the art which best expressed that meaning. The ancient Hebrews, for example, believed that there is one God and that the meaning of life consists in conforming to his will. Consequently, the art of the Hebrews, as one finds it in the Psalms, the words of the prophets, or the book of Genesis, was intended to express that attitude. Where it succeeded, it was good; where it failed, bad. For the Greeks, by contrast, the meaning of life lay in strength, vitality and happiness. Thus, for them, the purpose of art was to transmit energy and joy in living. That art was good which itself had energy or vitality and bad where it lacked those qualities or transmitted contrary ones. Amongst the Romans what was of paramount importance was national glory; amongst the Chinese it was exaltation of one's ancestors and maintenance of their traditions. Hence it was these ideals which Roman and Chinese artists sought to transmit. The aim of Buddhism is to free oneself from attachment to the bodily passions. Consequently, art which exalted the soul and humbled the flesh was good and art which strengthened the bodily passions was bad.

Throughout the ancient world, therefore, one finds that what is good or bad in the art of a society is determined by what is considered to be fundamentally important for the society as a whole.

Tolstoy now turns to the relation between art and society in the Christian era. As we have noted, he has his own interpretation of Christianity and this figures prominently in his account. Amongst the early Christians, he says, art was marked by its simplicity. The supreme examples are found in the Gospels, in their stories and parables, which served Tolstoy in his later period as models of great art. Their greatness consists precisely in their combination of simplicity and profundity. They embody wisdom which is immediately accessible alike to the learned and the unlearned. A similar simplicity, according to Tolstoy, characterized the whole art of the early Christians. He says, for example, that they rejected the visual arts except where these had a symbolic value in representing truths of the faith. In their sermons, prayers and hymns they confined themselves to evoking the love of Christ, humility and the love of others.

On Tolstoy's view, a change occurred in Christianity after the development of an organized Church and especially after Christianity was adopted by the Roman Empire. This involved the incorporation into Christianity of elements that belonged to pagan society, the society of the Greeks and Romans. For example, in early Christianity devotion is confined to Christ; but in later Christianity it is extended to the Virgin Mary, angels, apostles and martyrs. Similarly, there is a growing complexity in Christian art. The visual arts, for example, are now brought into full play. This development is seen especially in the Middle Ages, with the building of vast cathedrals, lavishly decorated with sculpture and painting.

Nevertheless Christian art during this period had one great virtue. It gave expression to beliefs and feelings that were genuinely held, not simply by the artists themselves but by the whole community. Therefore, says Tolstoy, it was true art:

> The teaching on the basis of which this art arose was a perversion of Christ's teaching but the art which sprang up on this perverse teaching was for all that a true art, since it corresponded to the religious view of life held by the people among whom it arose.
> The artists of the Middle Ages, vitalized by the same source of feeling – religion – as the mass of the people, and transmitting in architecture, sculpture, painting, music, poetry, or drama, the feelings and states of mind they experienced, were true artists; and their activity, founded on the highest conceptions accessible to their age and common to the entire people -though for our times a mean art – was nevertheless a true art, shared by the whole community.[1]

Thus the change in art, during the Middle Ages, though real, was not radical. But there occurred a radical change, according to Tolstoy, during the course of the eighteenth century. This arose through a growth of scepticism among the richer and more educated members of society. The scepticism itself had a variety of causes, such as the development of a scientific view of the world and the criticism, often legitimate, of medieval Christianity. It was a scepticism, however, that was confined to the upper classes. The mass of people retained their allegiance to Christianity. Moreover, the upper classes, having lost their faith in Christianity, did not replace it with another faith. Quite the contrary, they maintained a façade of belief, holding that an explicit repudiation of Christianity would endanger their own position and privileges.

Tolstoy now argues that the decadence of art in his own time has its source in this division. The upper classes were the chief patrons of the sophisticated arts. Consequently the sophisticated arts reflected their interests rather than those of the people. The effect was to trivialize the arts, since the interests thus reflected belonged to people who no longer held any profound belief. What they required of art was that it should entertain and flatter them. This was an art that could truly be defined as having pleasure as its aim but only because it has lost any vital function in society as a whole.

The philosophies of art which flourished in the eighteenth and nineteenth centuries were fitted to the situation which had arisen. Confronted by an art which had lost its function, they attempted to find it a purpose within itself. In consequence we find aesthetic theories defining art in terms of beauty. Here Tolstoy is on old ground. To affirm that an object is beautiful is to affirm that it affords a certain kind of pleasure. It produces what is pleasant to see, to hear or to read. In short, the definition is in subjective terms, art being viewed as mere consumption. It is the view of the idle spectator. As such it is well fitted to serve the interests of the leisure classes.

Tolstoy elaborates his point by making an acute criticism of the distinctions, common in the eighteenth and nineteenth centuries, between truth, goodness and beauty. It was commonly held that each of these was pursued by a separate branch of culture. Truth was the object of science, goodness that of morality and beauty that of art. The effect of this is to isolate both art and science from goodness. Tolstoy, by contrast, argues that goodness is predominant in all branches of culture. The point is central to his argument. To separate a culture into different segments is to destroy that culture, for there is no genuine culture without a unity. But there is no unity without a sense, pervasive in the culture, of what is important in life, in short, of what is good. Tolstoy acknowledges that beauty has been important in some cultures. He takes as an instance the importance of physical beauty in Greek art. He argues, however, that beauty was important in Greek art because it was important in Greek culture, not because it was an end confined to art alone. It was the expression in Greek art of that joy in vitality and health which Tolstoy takes to have been characteristic of the culture as a whole. In other words, it was the expression in art of what the Greeks found good in life. The point applies equally to science. For example, the aim of science cannot be simply the truth. For much truth is trivial. No scientist occupies himself in counting the grains of sand on the sea shore. Science is concerned only with truth which is valuable, important or good. What applies to science applies even more evidently to art. Thus the aim of art is not to provide whatever is found pleasant or beautiful, but to provide food or sustenance for the soul. Consequently its aim is to provide only what it is *good* to find pleasant or beautiful.

Tolstoy's account, so far, has been pessimistic. He has described how during the eighteenth century, through the influence of the upper classes, art has been diverted from its true purposes, resulting in a decadence of the arts. But he is not pessimistic in general. The attitude of the upper classes he treats as an aberration. They stand outside the line of human advance. Consequently their influence, though serious, is not fatal. Tolstoy believes that through the centuries Christianity has been undergoing a purification from the corruptions introduced under the Roman Empire. The upper classes are at fault because they have ignored this advance. They have often been correct in their criticism of the Catholic Church. But they have ignored the reformations of the Protestants, who in their worship have removed the corruptions of the Catholic Church and have returned to the simplicity found among the early Christians. Tolstoy did not count himself among the Protestants, for they had retained certain dogmas, such as that of the Trinity or of the Incarnation, which he considered inessential. For him, as we have seen, the essence of Christianity lies in the love of God, the fellowship of human beings, the rejection of worldly values and the development of humility and love. Nevertheless he treats the Protestant Reformation as a stage in the purification of Christianity and he believes this purification will continue and develop. In a society pervaded by the spirit of true Christianity, Tolstoy sees the basis for a purified art.

We have already remarked on the influence which the Enlightenment had on Tolstoy's thought. We noted also that he continued to be influenced by its attitudes even when he had rejected many of its explicit doctrines. Both these points are evident in the above account. For example, Tolstoy attributes the decadence of art, at least in its early stages, to the scepticism that had arisen among educated people in the eighteenth century. These are precisely the people who had been influenced by the leading figures of the Enlightenment. Yet in his very criticism of these figures Tolstoy betrays their influence. The Enlightenment view of society is sometimes termed voluntarism. Crudely put, voluntarism is the view that if something goes wrong there must be someone to blame for it. More formally put, it is the view that since society is merely a collection of individuals, whatever occurs in society must be explicable by reference to what individuals will. It is this attitude that Tolstoy exhibits in criticizing the Enlightenment itself. He assumes that someone must be blamed for the decadence of art and he puts all the blame on the wealthy and educated sceptics of the eighteenth century.

Voluntarism became old-fashioned during the course of the nineteenth century. There was an increasing awareness that social forces are not explicable, in any simple fashion, by reference to what individuals will. We mentioned, for example, the effect on the nineteenth century of the French Revolution and the development of industrialization. The French Revolution cannot be explained without reference to the wills or intentions of those who initiated it. But its consequences cannot be explained wholly in those terms, for in many cases they were the opposite of what was intended. Moreover, the consequences had their effect on the wills or intentions of particular individuals, making them different from what they otherwise might have been. Similarly, the process of industrialization involved the wills or intentions of particular industrialists. But the system of industrialization which arose out of their efforts was not intended by any of them. Their efforts were directed not towards the development of an industrial system but towards their own profit. The system arose out of the adjustments which, in pursuit of their profit, they made one to the other. It was the result of their activity but not of their conscious intention. So obvious did these points become by the close of the century that theorists moved to a view at the opposite extreme from that of the Enlightenment. Herbert Spencer, for example, argued that the social process had its own laws, which resisted conscious manipulation or control. Thus government interference in the economy would not only fail in its attempts but would make matters worse than they were before.[2] This was the famous doctrine of *laissez-faire*. It reappeared in the 1970s and 1980s, when it was proclaimed as a truth hitherto unknown to the human species. It was a commonplace in the 1890s. It disappeared in the first half of the twentieth century. But that was because, in the mean time, people had had direct experience of its consequences. This doctrine illustrates the tendency of the human mind to react against one error by embracing an error on the opposite side, while missing the truth in between. Thus the error of the Enlightenment was not to suppose that under certain conditions one may exert control over the social process, sometimes for the better. The error – or, better, delusion – was to suppose that human beings can exert such control over social conditions as to change them for the better, *whenever they put their minds to it*. They lacked the sense of any check on human improvement other than the errors or wickedness of particular individuals and therefore supposed progress inevitable, once these were exposed.

The same tendency appears in Tolstoy's account. We have noted that the role of the artist in nineteenth-century society was profoundly affected by such events as the French Revolution and the process of industrialization. These events do not figure in Tolstoy's account. Like the thinkers of the Enlightenment, having detected an evil he is anxious to put the blame or responsibility on some group of individuals. In consequence, he passes over causes which lie more deeply in the social process. We shall note the same tendency when he proceeds to discuss the artists of his own time. For example, he blames the writers of his time for their lack of clarity, the assumption being that they write in that way from perversity, simply choosing to disregard their audience. He does not consider that they may lack an audience, through circumstances over which they have little control, and that some of them, at least, may deserve credit for writing as well as they can in the circumstances.

The influence of the Enlightenment is seen also in Tolstoy's progressivism. In the history of Europe, as we have noted, he finds the record of human advance. The evils of his own time he treats as an aberration. They are outside the line of that advance. He is confident, therefore, that Christianity will be purified of its corruptions and will increase its influence, this resulting in the purification of the arts. None of this has occurred. Indeed, what has occurred is the opposite of what he predicted. We find, for example, that the attitudes which Tolstoy condemned in the leisure classes, so far from disappearing, have become more pervasive. In the Western industrial countries, they have spread to the whole population. Thus Christianity, so far from increasing its influence, has steadily declined. The revival of the economy after the Second World War has increased wealth throughout most sections of society. The artist, therefore, has a large and wealthy audience to whom he can appeal on the free market. But the audience to whom he appeals is no more united in fundamental belief than were the leisure classes of Tolstoy's day. Consequently, in order to be successful he has to produce whatever satisfies his public at any give time. The criterion of success is what satisfies, what appeals, what gives pleasure. It will be noticed that this was precisely the criterion that Tolstoy condemned. The artist may avoid the free market, surviving on grants from various organizations. But then he will be in the position of so many a sophisticated artist in the late nineteenth century. In short, he will lack an audience.

But we must remember that Tolstoy, though he has simplified the causes, may still have diagnosed the disease. His account, though historical in form, is not historical in its purpose. His purpose is to reveal the condition of art in his own time by a contrast with earlier societies where, in his view, it has flourished. In the chapters which follow he proceeds to a more direct study of art in his own time, indicating those of its features that he considers decadent

## Notes

1 *What is Art?*, pp. 130–31.
2 See H. Spencer, *The Man Versus The State*, Harmondsworth, Penguin, 1969. It is worth noting that this book does not represent the whole of Spencer's thought. He was one of the most impressive of Victorian thinkers and has been unjustly neglected.

CHAPTER SEVEN

# Decadent Art

Tolstoy has specified the conditions which lead to decadence in art and, by contrast, those which are propitious for its flourishing. It flourishes when it has its roots in beliefs that are fundamental to the life of a people, these being religious in the sense that they give expression to what for that people is the meaning of life. It becomes decadent when it is cut off from those roots. He now spends a number of chapters (from the eighth to the fifteenth) indicating the marks or distinctive features of decadent art. He distinguishes three such marks. The first is that decadent art appeals only to a small section of society, such as the wealthy or leisured. The second is that it has a narrow range of themes, the chief being flattery of the wealthy and powerful, sexual attraction and that boredom or discontent with life which is characteristic of the leisured class. The third is that it cultivates obscurity and complexity of style.

To illustrate these points, and especially the last, Tolstoy proceeds in several chapters to consider some of the artists prominent in his time. These chapters are perhaps the most notorious in his book. Tolstoy caused resentment by attacking some of the most respected artists of his age. He caused resentment, also, by attacking one of the central conceptions of Romantic art. We have noted Gautier's view that artists have no responsibility to a public, their aim being to cultivate beauty. Tolstoy makes clear that an artist who feels no responsibility to a public, who has no wish to communicate, has no right to call himself an artist.

The resentment which Tolstoy caused was in some respects justified. In controversy, as we have said, he was often impatient and sometimes unjust. He was inclined, also, to the besetting sin of the controversialist. In the heat of controversy he swings to a view at the opposite extreme from the one he is attacking. The point is evident in his attack on the Romantic conception of art. Reading, perhaps with sympathy, his criticism of the view that the artist has no obligation to communicate with a public, one is suddenly aware that he is now at an opposite extreme. It now appears that the responsibility for communicating with a public lies *wholly* with the artist. It is the obligation of the artist to capture the attention of the public. The public, apparently, have no duty to attend. Since communication requires two sides, one would have thought that responsibilities should fall on both of the sides involved.

But we must ourselves beware of falling into the sin which besets critics of Tolstoy. This consists in treating whatever weakness he shows as a major one. We shall find that his faults in criticizing others do little to undermine his central account of what is important in art. Tolstoy at his worst is often inconsistent with what he himself holds when he is at his best.

Let us begin, however, with the weak side of his criticism. We shall take two examples. The first is his criticism of Charles Baudelaire, perhaps the most famous French poet of the late nineteenth century. Tolstoy takes Baudelaire's poetry as a prime example of decadent art, emphasizing the obscurity of its style and the degraded nature of its themes. Anyone who is familiar with Baudelaire's poetry will be forced to acknowledge that it exhibits some of the features which Tolstoy attributes to a decadent art. For example, it is often concerned with sexual desire; it frequently expresses boredom and discontent and it is preoccupied with various forms of evil. It is also urban in its setting, dealing with themes which will be familiar to people who live in cities rather than on the land. Moreover, it could be described as obscure, at least when judged by the standards of the folk tale or the parables in the Gospels.

But there are respects, also, in which it differs from decadent art, as Tolstoy describes it. For example, it is hardly designed to flatter the idle rich. Its very difficulty or obscurity seems to make that unlikely. Tolstoy says that decadent art caters to the rich and idle and also that it revels in obscurity. But this seems inconsistent. For why should the rich, any more than the rest of us, be especially attracted to the obscure or difficult? If they are as idle as Tolstoy claims, we should expect them to prefer literature which is light, amusing and superficial. But Baudelaire's poetry has none of these features.

What is even more important is the way Baudelaire handles his themes. It is true that he is preoccupied with evil. Nevertheless it appears *as* evil. Goodness is indirectly present, because evil appears as it really is. We are aware that sin is sin and not a higher form of goodness. Indeed, there are passages in Baudelaire that have a parallel in the works of the great Christian writers, who have never been afraid to characterize the features of evil. In short, there is a suspicion that Tolstoy is slipping into a crude form of didacticism, judging a work by its overt subject matter rather than by its overall effect. This is contrary to his theory. But Tolstoy's theory was sometimes in conflict with his practice.

We may note a final weakness in his criticism of Baudelaire. As we have said, Baudelaire's themes are urban. At any rate, they are more readily appreciated by the city dweller than by the peasant, to whom in many respects they may seem unintelligible. That, of course, would be one of Tolstoy's grounds for complaint. But Baudelaire was hardly being perverse or eccentric in choosing such themes.[1] In many European countries, increasingly large numbers of people were becoming city-dwellers. Between these people and those who lived in the old way, there were striking differences in type of life. Where people live in very different ways it will be difficult, if not impossible, to write in ways that are immediately intelligible to everyone. Moreover, the fault seems evidently to lie as much with the social conditions in which the artist writes as with the artist himself.

Here we touch again on Tolstoy's insensitivity to certain social conditions. He too readily assumes in existence of the popular culture characteristic of

Europe in the past, whereas in fact many people were losing contact with that culture and were moving to cities where there was no culture to replace it. Having no universal culture to appeal to, the artist was confronted by formidable difficulties. So far as these difficulties could be overcome, an effort was required not simply by the artist but also by his audience. The audience could not reasonably expect the artist to communicate in the simple and direct manner which was possible in a peasant culture. It is true that where conditions become this complicated, they offer a special opportunity to the charlatan. Tolstoy was correct in claiming that many artists took advantage of the situation to revel in obscurity. But there were genuine artists as well as charlatans and he was sometimes too impatient to distinguish between the two.

We may take a second example to illustrate that point. Towards the middle of his tenth chapter, Tolstoy moves away from literature and considers the visual arts. He there gives an account of an exhibition that was held by the group of artists who became known as the Impressionists. His account was based on one given by his daughter, who at the time was a student of art:

> In the same gallery ... were other pictures: by Puvis de Chavannes, Manet, Monet, Renoir, Sisley, who are all Impressionists. One of them, whose name I could not make out – it was something like Redon – had painted a blue face in profile. On the whole face there is only this blue tone with white-of-lead. Pissarro has a water-colour all done with dots. In the foreground is a cow entirely painted with various-coloured dots. The general colour cannot be distinguished, however much one stands back from, or draws near to, the picture.[2]

The description is given at some length, expressing throughout an incomprehension of the pictures on display. The reaction is perfectly honest and at the time was widely shared, not only by the general public but also by trained artists. Tolstoy takes for granted that the reaction is sound and that the artists on display are simply charlatans. Now the Impressionists, those on display, are in fact an excellent example of the type of artist who at first is difficult to understand, becomes with a little effort less difficult and eventually becomes entirely comprehensible. In their case, the public soon discovered that their style of painting was not perverse but was adopted because it enabled them to obtain certain effects, especially effects of light, which could not have been obtained in any other way. Moreover, in order to appreciate this it was not necessary to be a trained artist. The Impressionists were among the last artists of modern times, of a sophisticated kind, to be assimilated by the popular understanding, so that one will find reproductions of paintings by Renoir or Monet or Pissarro hanging in shops, public houses, schools, offices and people's homes.

We must turn now from the weak to the strong side of Tolstoy's account. So far, he has specified the following features of decadent art: it appeals only to a limited audience; it has a limited subject matter; it is lacking in clarity. He now turns to a question which may have occurred already to his readers. If the art to which he refers is as bad as he implies, why does it have an appeal at all? The artists he mentions may not have a wide audience but they certainly appeal to some people. In educated circles, some may be described as famous. Tolstoy has implied an answer, it is true, in suggesting that decadent artists flatter the rich. As we have seen, however, that answer is far from satisfactory. He now provides a better answer by analysing the techniques on which decadent art depends for its appeal. What he says is of great interest not simply in itself but also for the fresh light it sheds on his positive view of art. We must consider it in some detail.

What Tolstoy seeks to show is that decadent art depends for its appeal on a set of techniques or devices which are really inartistic, which stand to genuine art as a kind of counterfeit. To see how these devices arise, we must recollect that the requirements for genuine art are complex. Thus an artist must have something *worthwhile to communicate*; he must *want* to communicate it; he must have the *ability*, in words or sounds or paint, to infect an audience with what he wants to communicate, in short, he must have *talent*. Now it often happens that some of these conditions are present without the others. For example, a person may be fluent in words, or have a good sense of pitch, or a knack for drawing – in short, have talent – and yet have nothing worthwhile to communicate with his gift. Nevertheless he may still wish to be an artist, either because he does not know he has nothing worthwhile to communicate or because he is simply interested in money and fame. How then might he proceed? In his eleventh chapter, Tolstoy indicates four ways in which he might do so.

(*a*) The first and most obvious device is that of *borrowing*. One notices the works having an effect and reproduces their features. Someone who is talented can in this way produce work which is technically good. Nevertheless, work produced in this way is hollow, not so much because the artist is copying another person's style as because he has nothing of his own to say in the style he has copied. What he has produced is really counterfeit art.

(*b*) The second feature is what Tolstoy calls *imitation*. He means the imitation of social life or the natural world, not of other artists. He probably had in mind the vogue in the late nineteenth century for the so-called naturalistic novel. This was the type of novel that aimed to represent some section of society in copious and realistic detail. To illustrate why Tolstoy thought this genre tended to the counterfeit, let us take an imaginary example. Suppose I have a gift for words and I write a novel giving a vivid representation of life in the university where I work. You may be sure that those who work in this university will have an interest in reading it. It is possible, of course, that I might have produced a genuine work of art. The point is, however, that it does not have to be a genuine work of art in order to interest those who work in my university. People like to be reminded of scenes or incidents in which they have been involved. There is nothing wrong with this in itself. Tolstoy's point, however, is that the work which caters simply to this interest is not genuinely artistic. Genuine art *enlarges* our interest; it does not simply remind us of what we have experienced already. Thus the realistic or imitative novel is counterfeit so far as it simply relies on an interest which is supplied by its audience. A related phenomenon may be found in numerous bookshops. Many of the books most prominently on display are written not by artists but by sportsmen, film stars, politicians and soldiers. In short, what attracts people to these works is their subject matter rather than its re-creation in art.

Imitative art, then, is counterfeit because it relies entirely on the interest or experience which the audience brings to it. Genuine art, by contrast, enlarges the audience's interest or experience. But to achieve this the artist needs more than talent; he must have something fresh or new to communicate. It is important to note, however, that what is fresh or new need not be something altogether unprecedented. Art enlarges our experience not simply by recreating for us experiences hitherto unknown but also by recreating aspects hitherto unnoticed in what lies within our experience. Tolstoy himself, some years before, had supplied an example in *Anna Karenina*. Vronsky, Anna's lover, has commissioned a portrait of her from the artist Mihailov:

> After the fifth sitting the portrait impressed everybody, especially Vronsky, not only by its likeness but also by its peculiar beauty. It was strange how Mihailov had been able to discover that peculiar beauty. 'One needs to know her and love her, as I have loved her, to discover the very sweetest expression of her soul', thought Vronsky, though it was only through this portrait that he himself learned this sweetest expression of her soul. But the expression was so true that it seemed to him, and to others, too, that they had always known it.[3]

It is worth noting also, though at the risk of becoming tedious, that these passages, yet again, are in conflict with the interpretation of Tolstoy as an extreme didacticist. The essence of didacticism is that it treats the value of art as lying wholly or largely in its subject matter. It is precisely this feature that Tolstoy here takes as a mark of counterfeit art. In genuine art, by contrast, the artist has revealed something fresh or new through the artistic treatment of his subject matter.

(c) The third feature, which Tolstoy takes as a mark of decadent art, he calls the *striking device*. The characteristic of such a device is that it creates an effect by breaking violently with accepted form. One of the most famous examples occurs in Beethoven's Third Symphony, the 'Eroica'. In the first movement, as the music reaches a climax, a horn blares forth on a discordant note. It is said that Beethoven's nephew, when he first heard the music, assumed the horn player had made a mistake. In fact he was playing just what Beethoven had written. Here we have a departure from accepted form so extreme that a normal listener may be unsure whether or not it is intended. Similar devices appear in the music of other composers during the Romantic period, such as Berlioz and Liszt.

Now for Tolstoy these devices are counterfeit, because they exploit the appeal of extreme sound at the expense of musical form. Tolstoy calls this appeal physical rather than musical. Any loud sound, for example, suddenly occurring when one has experienced and anticipates silence, will set the nerves jangling and will strike one as startling, frightening, dramatic. A similar effect can be achieved in music by introducing a dissonance where the audience anticipates harmony. But that for Tolstoy is not music. In genuine music every note derives its force from its relation to other notes within an overall structure. It does not work by arbitrary effects, however dramatic or startling they may be in themselves.

In fact this criticism is unjust when it is applied to composers in the early Romantic period. For their extreme devices were not arbitrary but had an expressive function within the work as a whole. Such devices, for example, can serve to express extreme states, such as grief, despair or horror, and may therefore contribute to the emotional quality of the overall work. But Tolstoy's criticism is by no means unjust when applied to composers of a later date. As the century developed, composers made increasing use of extreme sounds. This was connected with the development of the orchestra. During the course of the nineteenth century, the orchestra grew in size and also in the power of its instruments, so that it could produce a body of sound hitherto unknown. Composers increasingly exploited its resources. As Tolstoy suggests, the effect was especially evident in opera, a subject to which we shall return in some detail. In the eighteenth and early nineteenth centuries, the events in an opera were expressed primarily through melodic writing for the voice, the orchestra serving merely as support or accompaniment. By the middle of the nineteenth century, however, the orchestra had often become the centre of interest. It was used not simply to produce effects which the voice could not produce, such as those of a storm or a battle, but also to express emotions such as grief or love, hitherto expressed by the voice alone.

Now these developments led by the turn of the century to a crisis in music. The crisis is too complicated for us to consider in detail. But some features stand out. Return for a moment to the effect of a loud sound and it will be evident that it is subject to the law of diminishing returns. It is not as startling on the second occasion as on the first. To obtain the same effect, you have to increase the sound and you have to continue increasing it on every subsequent occasion. Now, similarly, an effect which could be obtained early in the nineteenth century by a modest increase in sound could be obtained by the end of the century only through the united efforts of a whole orchestra. Moreover, the use of extreme devices in early Romantic music presupposed the background of a common musical form. It was by a contrast with this background that it obtained its effects. The continued and proliferating use of these devices destroyed the sense of a common form. But in so doing it destroyed the contrast on which it depended for an effect. Here we have a dramatic illustration of Tolstoy's theme, of the relation between the use of counterfeit devices and decadence, the decay or decline of an art.

We have concentrated on music in order to illustrate what Tolstoy means by the striking device. But in fact, as he insists, it may be found in all the arts. In our own time, we may note, for example, the use in the cinema of extreme violence. Thus a director will show a brutal killing in horrific detail not because it is required by the story but because he knows it will shock or disrupt his audience. The use of sex is equally obvious.

(*d*) The fourth feature of decadent art which Tolstoy distinguishes is that of *interesting or intriguing the audience*. This is fairly straightforward. For example, some dramatists are good at concocting clever or intriguing plots. They keep you guessing as to who committed the murder and it turns out to be someone you did not suspect. This device diverts the mind but does not enlighten it. Obscurity of style performs a similar function at a more sophisticated level. You are left to guess what the author means, this affording the type of amusement that is found in solving a puzzle. Again, there may be nothing wrong with amusing puzzles. But for Tolstoy they are not art, because the person who concocts them has nothing to reveal about life.

Reflecting on Tolstoy's account of the devices used in counterfeit art, one may be struck by the balance he keeps between the Romantic and the Classical. Tolstoy's view of art is akin to the Romantic in valuing originality and expressiveness. But it is Classical in the importance it gives to form. John Bayley, in his study *Tolstoy and the Novel*, mentions as one of Tolstoy's most striking qualities his fastidiousness.[4] He gives as evidence Tolstoy's embarrassment and shame when confronted by the crude or theatrical effects which, by his time, had become common in the public or performing arts.[5] The theatrical effect is one designed to impress the audience at any price. The artist has his eye more on his audience than on his material and he will make whatever adjustment in his material is needed to meet their approval. For Tolstoy, that is the opposite of genuine art. In genuine art, the artist is preoccupied with giving his material aesthetic *form*. It is through the form he gives his material that he affects his audience. Tolstoy calls this artistic *sincerity*. In insincere or counterfeit art, the effects are aimed simply at pleasing an audience. In sincere or genuine art, the aim is to impress an audience through the adequacy of its effects to its material. We shall return, in a later chapter, to the idea of sincerity in art

Tolstoy next turns to the forms of organization which encourage the production of counterfeit art. He considers, in particular, the training of artists in art schools and music colleges, the role of professionalism in the arts and the place of critics. It will be useful to concentrate on what he says about training in the arts, because this will enable us to elaborate on the remarks made above.

Tolstoy's chief complaint against art schools and music colleges is that they can communicate only general techniques and not what is most important in art. Indeed, it is not simply that they cannot communicate what is most important; what they do communicate are just those techniques most readily adapted to produce counterfeit art. He does not mean, however, that general techniques or rules have no place at all in genuine art but rather that they cannot produce it. He gives an example to illustrate his meaning. The artist Bryulóv once corrected a pupil's drawing by adding to it a few touches. The student remarked that although he had added only a few tiny details, the drawing was entirely transformed. Bryulóv replied that it is in the tiny details that art resides. In short, the details which make a particular work successful are too fine to be covered by a general formula. They are the details which are particular to *this* work; one will not find them by searching among others.[6] We may note that Bryulóv's remark applies to a skill or craft and not simply to the fine arts. For example, two cooks who are correctly following exactly the same recipe may still produce different dishes. One, for example, may be much better than the other. That is because a supremely good dish also depends on details which are too fine to be covered by a general formula. They are achieved only by those who have developed a feeling for their work and are no longer guided by external rules. It does not follow that rules are unnecessary in cookery. But the supreme exponents have so absorbed them that they no longer need to follow them in conscious thought and can therefore concentrate wholly on the task at hand.

Moreover, if this is true of a skill or craft, it is more evidently true of the fine arts. Thus the details which bring a work alive are found by the artist who has so absorbed the techniques of his art that he no longer needs to think about them and can concentrate wholly on what he wishes to communicate. In this way, he achieves what is personal, original, distinctive. Note, however, that he achieves originality through absorption in his art, not by aiming at originality itself. The artist who aims consciously at originality is viewing his work externally. He has his eye not on his work but on other artists, from whom he wishes to differ. In this respect, he is as much dominated by fashion as is the mere imitator. The latter in his work copies other artists; the former in his differs from them. But both are dominated in their work by other artists. The genuine artist is wholly preoccupied with what he wishes to communicate. In this way, he achieves originality without having to aim at it. A false conception of originality was a potent cause of decadence in late Romantic art. Here, again, we see the Classical base of Tolstoy's account.

Tolstoy's criticism of the art of his contemporaries is not complete. He has reserved a separate chapter for the leading composer of his time, Richard Wagner, whom he takes as typifying its decadence. We shall consider in some detail what he has to say.

### Notes

1 In this respect, see the discussion of Baudelaire in Walter Benjamin, *Illuminations*, London, Pimlico, 1999, pp. 152–97.
2 *What is Art?*, p. 171.

3 *Anna Karenina*, London, Penguin Books, 1978, p. 503.
4 J. Bayley, *Tolstoy and the Novel*, London, Chatto and Windus, 1966, p. 245.
5 See, for example, *What is Art?*, p. 212.
6 The reader may here recall a passage quoted by Long, 'A Selective Defence', pp. 47–8.

CHAPTER EIGHT

# Wagner

Richard Wagner was the most influential composer in Europe when Tolstoy was writing *What is Art?* and, next to Beethoven, he remains the most famous composer of his century. Tolstoy's wholehearted attack on this figure is, again, notorious, being widely considered perverse, both in its judgements and in the method of its criticism. In its method of criticism, there are certainly perversities. It remains to be seen whether they invalidate the criticism as a whole. Let us begin with some details of Wagner's life.

Wagner lived from 1813 to 1883. His formal training in music was very slight, lasting for little more than a year. But there was a love of music in his family and also an interest in the theatre. His stepfather was a minor actor and dramatist. Music and the theatre were Wagner's abiding passions and of the two, at least in his earlier years, it was the theatre which was predominant. As we shall see, he formed a theory according to which not simply music but every art can achieve its supreme expression only in the context of a drama. He rapidly acquired a knowledge, eventually a mastery, both of the orchestra and of the techniques involved in dramatic performance. The other passion of his youth was revolutionary politics. He caught the excitement produced among intellectuals by the French Revolution and shared their hope in a revolutionary transformation of society. His view of art was related to that hope. Like many another artist at the time, he believed that art, by expressing the spirit of a new and better society would help in inspiring people to bring that society about and would therefore itself serve a political role. His political hopes faded, but throughout his life he retained his progressive view of art. For him, the greatest artist is the one who is in advance of his age, having divined the music of the future. This he can do by divining the spirit of a people, of which they themselves are not fully aware, but of which he is fully aware and which he can realize by giving it expression in his art. His political views he put into effect in 1849, at Dresden, where he stood at the barricades alongside the famous anarchist Bakunin, whom he greatly admired. The revolution in Dresden was not successful and he had to flee the country. For a while, he hoped that a revolution would occur in France, where he had taken refuge. When he was disappointed in this, he became pessimistic about politics and thereafter devoted himself entirely to art.

Before the revolution, Wagner had already achieved some success in opera. Three of the works he wrote at the time have retained a place in the repertoire – *The Flying Dutchman*, *Tannhäuser* and *Lohengrin*. In these works, however, he had to some extent compromised with the commercial theatre. For some years after the revolution, he ceased to compose, devoting himself to prose writings in which he advocated his ideas for a radically new type of drama. It was on the basis of these ideas that he composed his later and most famous works, such as *Tristan and Isolde* and *The Ring of the Nibelungen*. In these works all compromise with the commercial theatre is abandoned. *The Ring*, for example, is an immense drama which takes the better part of a week to stage. It is framed as a trilogy with a prelude, but the prelude is itself the length of a standard opera. Wagner, however, was rescued from having to rely on the commercial theatre by the patronage of King Ludwig of Bavaria, who allowed him a free hand to fulfil his artistic desires. Eventually Wagner built a theatre, at Bayreuth, which was devoted to his own work and has remained a centre for his followers.

Wagner was a voluminous writer. He was also the cause of much writing in others:

> No musician, perhaps no artist in the history of Western art, has ever had so much to say about his own life, works and ideas as did Richard Wagner. And with the possible exception of Beethoven, no musician has ever exercised such influence over men and even nations as has Wagner in the past one hundred years. In his own lifetime alone, Wagner was the subject of ten thousand articles and books, attacking, defending, and explaining his system and his cult.[1]

But Wagner, though a voluminous writer, was not a gifted one. The editors of a useful selection from his writings, for example, find themselves obliged to acknowledge his constitutional incapacity for simple and direct utterance, this being partly a vice of his nation and period but partly also a flaw in his own mind.[2] His writings come alive when he discusses the details of a musical or dramatic performance. Otherwise he exhibits that most distressing feature of the second rate thinker – his ideas are a mere reflection of whatever passes in his own time as original or advanced.

We may trace on his ideas three types of influence. The first is the writings of the revolutionaries. Commerce, gold, represented for Wagner by the Jew, dominant in his society, are a potent source of corruption in its art. The transformation of art requires, therefore, its freedom from the commercial spirit.

The second influence lies in that attitude to history which had become common among advanced thinkers since the Enlightenment. As we have noted, it is found also in Tolstoy. Between Ancient Greece and the Renaissance, we are told, there lies a cultural wasteland. The cause may be found in the dominance of the Catholic Church, whose doctrines are a mere perversion of Christ's teaching. Wagner differs from Tolstoy over when the perversion first arose. For Tolstoy it was when Christianity was adopted by the Roman Empire. For Wagner it virtually coincided with the appearance of Christianity itself, the cause of the mischief being St Paul. Through St Paul's influence, spirit was divorced from body, the idea of sin became dominant, and people were deprived of a free and joyous existence. The contrast with Ancient Greece is apparent. The very idea of sin, as Christianity conceives of it, was alien to the Greeks, whose ideal was a life joyous, sensuous and free. At this point it is easy to anticipate Wagner's view that a transformation of the arts, in his time, requires a recovery of the Greek spirit.

The third influence came from the leading German thinkers of the Romantic period. Johann Gottlieb Fichte is here the central influence; but to understand his thought we need to consider the assumptions he and his contemporaries inherited from Kant. In his *Critique of Pure Reason*, Kant had analysed what he called speculative metaphysics. The speculative metaphysician is one who attempts through pure or contemplative reason to grasp the ultimate nature of reality and to reveal it in the form of a complete system. Plato and Spinoza are usually cited as examples. But in fact, on Kant's analysis, the greater part of traditional philosophy consists of speculative metaphysics. In his *Critique*, Kant argued that the whole enterprise is misguided. Reason, though it cannot be reduced to sense experience, is limited by sense experience in its working. This means that it cannot transcend the empirical world and that the only genuine form of knowledge is empirical science. Through knowledge, therefore, we can never obtain a contact with ultimate reality. Nevertheless, what cannot be obtained through knowledge may in a manner be obtained through faith and action. In moral action, especially, we exhibit, though we cannot understand, a realm of freedom which transcends the empirical.

Kant's account of the history of philosophy has been enormously influential. For some two centuries, indeed, it has been the standard account. Nevertheless it is a mere travesty of the facts. Plato, for example, never set forth a system of philosophy. His works are dialectical, written as dialogues, involving a conflict between different views. It is true that we have letters attributed to him. In the seventh, commonly accepted as genuine, he explicitly denies the possibility of a systematic philosophy. Moreover, one can suppose that he found the source of knowledge in pure or contemplative reason only by ignoring some of his most famous works. In the *Symposium* and the *Phaedrus*, for example, he finds the source of knowledge in a transmutation not simply of the feelings but of the erotic feelings. Spinoza said that God has an infinity of attributes of which the human mind can grasp *two*. In short, on his philosophy, the human mind will never grasp more than a fragment of reality. In traditional philosophy one will have difficulty finding even an approximation to what Kant calls speculative metaphysics. One will find an approximation only in the nineteenth, the succeeding century, as for example in the metaphysics of Hegel or of the scientific positivists. The proof of this may be found in a simple reflection. Before the nineteenth century almost every great philosopher was a religious believer. It would evidently be absurd in a religious believer to claim that he had obtained an exhaustive knowledge of reality as a whole, for he would have to claim not simply that he believed in God but that he thoroughly understood him

Fichte, however, accepted many of Kant's basic ideas, and especially his distinction between reason or knowledge on the one hand and faith or action on the other. He elaborated this distinction, claiming that life begins in action, not in reason. Reason is an instrument provided by nature to make action effective. The world therefore cannot be understood through pure or contemplative reason. It is a dynamic rather than a static system; it is spirit rather than matter. The physical world is simply material for the activity of the spirit. Only those who unite themselves with the spirit of the world can know it. This requires faith. For one cannot first know the spirit of the world and then act. Only those who have the faith to act in the world can know that they are united with its spirit. Individuals may be distinguished according to whether or not they have this faith:

> Either you believe in an original principle in man – freedom, a perfectibility, an infinite progress of our species – or you believe in none of this. You may even have a feeling or some kind of intuition of its opposite. All those who have within them the creative quickening of life, or else, assuming that such a gift has been withheld from them, at least await the moment when they are caught up in the magnificent torrent of flowing and original life, or perhaps have some confused presentiment of such freedom, and have towards this phenomenon not hatred, nor fear, but a feeling of love, these are part of primal humanity ... All those, on the other hand, who have resigned themselves to represent only the derivatives, the second hand product, who think of themselves in this way, become such an effect, and shall pay the price of their belief. They are a mere annexe to life.[3]

What applies to individuals applies also to nations. In the winter of 1807–8, at Berlin, Fichte delivered a series of extraordinary addresses.[4] Berlin at the time was occupied by French forces. With remarkable courage, Fichte spoke out on behalf of the German nation. What he said helped, for more than a century, to form the consciousness of educated Germans. For example, a German philosopher of the twentieth century such as Martin Heidegger cannot be understood without some understanding of the attitude that Fichte expressed in these addresses.

Fichte argues that the moral regeneration of a nation is possible only where it has a free and living spirit capable of uniting its members. Such a spirit exists in the German people. They are pure and unmixed, having developed from a single stock. Their language has a wonderful plasticity, making it capable of giving concrete form to the profoundest thought. It was the ancient Germans who stemmed the tide of Roman domination; it was the Germans, again, who at the time of the Reformation purified religion. Only the Germans have proved their capacity for the deepest philosophical speculation. Consequently in language, religion and philosophy they prove themselves a free and living people. Fichte then proposes a scheme of national education, an indispensable requirement for the regeneration of the nation, and he makes clear that such a representation is of vital significance not simply for Germany but for Europe as a whole. All those who have a similar kinship with the world spirit are in essence Germans:

> All those who believe in spiritual reality, those who believe in the freedom of the life of the spirit ... whatever be their native land, whatever the language which they speak, they are our race, they are part of our people, or they will join it late or soon. All those who believe in arrested being, in retrogression, in eternal cycles, even those who believe in inanimate nature, and put her at the helm of the world, whatever be their native country, whatever be their language, they are not Germans, they are strangers to us, and one would hope that one day they would be wholly cut off from our people.[5]

One may have wondered why a nation such as the German, which is already in the spirit, needs to be regenerated. The above paragraph gives the answer. Not every member of such a nation will be in the spirit and not everyone who is in the spirit will be fully aware of it. In short, a nation has to be awakened to its destiny and inspired to follow it.

Now where Fichte speaks of national education as an agent of regeneration, Wagner speaks of art. As we have seen, Wagner holds that the people of Europe for many centuries were under the domination of the Church. He makes an exception, however, of one people:

> Nature is so strong, so inexhaustible in its regenerative resources, that no conceivable violence could weaken its creative force. Into the ebbing veins of the Roman world, there poured the healthy blood of the fresh Germanic nations. Despite the adoption of Christianity a ceaseless thirst of doing, delight in bold adventure, and unbounded self-reliance remained the native element of the new masters of the world.[6]

The spirit of Greece lives on, therefore, among the Germanic nations. Under modern conditions, however, that spirit is suppressed. Wagner now anticipates its regeneration in the art of the future. This will occur when art has the place in the life of a people that it had among the Greeks. For Wagner, the supreme expression of Greek art was the drama, as it was found, for example, in the tragedies of Aeschylus. In Greek drama the various arts were concentrated on *one* point. Employing poetry, music, sculpture, dance, painting, it gave expression in mythic form to the spirit of the Greek nation. With the decline of tragic drama, the arts became separated, each developing in its own way. Unity was lost.

Unity will be restored, on Wagner's view, in the art of the future. Opera will supply its basis, for it already combines various arts. Thus it evidently combines music and drama. Also, it requires stage effects which depend on painting, sculpture and the mechanical arts, and it needs to be housed, which involves architecture. In conventional opera, however, these arts are, as it were, simply juxtaposed. They lack genuine integration. In the new type of drama which Wagner envisages, the various arts will subserve a central conception that will transform them into a total work of art.

At Bayreuth, Wagner achieved much of what he envisaged. In conventional opera, the composer has his work staged at a theatre not specifically designed for it. Again, there is a division between composer and librettist, the one supplying the music, the other the words. In Wagnerian opera both words and music are written by Wagner himself. Moreover, the theatre at Bayreuth was designed specifically for his own works. He himself supervised the construction, every detail being designed to focus the attention of the audience on the stage. For example, to prevent their chatting, he had the seating so constructed that they were forced to look ahead. The orchestra was invisible, being sunk in a pit. During a performance, the lights were not dimmed, as was conventional, but switched off, so that only the stage was visible. The plot of a Wagnerian opera, though usually much longer than that of a naturalistic drama, is simpler in the sense that its characters are mythical and its action concentrated on two or three crucial scenes. By contrast, Wagner's stage effects were of the greatest possible elaboration, the mechanical arts being employed, for example, to produce fire-breathing dragons and Rhine maidens who really appeared to swim. In addition, he selected and rehearsed the singers, supervised and on occasions conducted the orchestra.

It is important to note, however, if we are to understand Wagner's later work, that his views underwent a change. We have seen that after the revolution at Dresden he became pessimistic about political activity. During the 1850s he became increasingly pessimistic not simply about political activity but in his view of life. To appreciate this, we must return for a moment to Fichte. As we have seen, Wagner in his earlier period shared Fichte's view that the spirit of the world is grasped not by contemplating the world but by acting within it. For Wagner, of course the spirit is essentially *immanent*. By this I mean that he had no belief in immortal life, except where that is a metaphor for some realm of joy and freedom which falls within history. This is evident in his revolutionary writings. The very aim of the revolution, as he envisaged it, was to achieve, as it were, a consummation of history. Through revolutionary activity, history would culminate in a realm of joy and freedom. In the 1850s, he came to believe that this view was illusory. Human action, whether on the individual or the political level, flows through the will from desire, but desire is insatiable. Any consummation it achieves will be temporary, leading to a renewal of desire. The only release from desire is in death. Wagner was influenced in this view by reading the works of Arthur Schopenhauer, another philosopher in the tradition of German Idealism. Schopenhauer is a complex and subtle philosopher.[7] But we are concerned not with his views themselves but with the way they were interpreted by Wagner. Wagner, in any case, claimed that Schopenhauer merely helped him to formulate views he had already grasped intuitively.

Under the influence of these views, Wagner moved to a position at the opposite extreme from Fichte's. The world is understood not in action but in contemplation. As Wagner put it in 1855, in a letter to Liszt, nature has fashioned the brain as an instrument for effective action; but in some individuals there is an excess of brain power. Nature has, as it were, over-reached itself, allowing to the exceptional individual an insight into its workings. To such an individual, it becomes evident that life is suffering. Ordinary individuals cannot realize this, because they believe that their suffering will be overcome when they achieve what they desire. They do not realize that their desire is itself the cause of their suffering, for it can never bring them permanent or lasting satisfaction. This insight is vouchsafed to the exceptional individual because, released for a moment from the flow of life, he is able to *contemplate* it. This contemplation is the only form of transcendence available to human beings. It is the basis of great art. There is grandeur in art because it transcends the purposes of life, not because it is effective in furthering them, and because it enables us, through that transcendence, to view life with pity and understanding.

The change in Wagner's view of life most evidently affects *The Ring*, for the change occurred while he was in the very process of writing it. He had intended a drama in which the hero, Siegfried, in the name of freedom and love, overcomes the corruption of the ruling powers, as represented by the gods. But the work turned, under his hand, into something quite different. The text was in fact complete before he studied Schopenhauer but the forces which made him receptive to Schopenhauer's philosophy must already have been at work. For in its completed form *The Ring* is an expression of human life in all its futility. The magic ring, which confers on its owner all worldly power, passes from hand to hand and returns at the end to the place from where it came, leaving in its wake total devastation. The grandeur of the work is supposed to lie not in the spectacle in itself but in its contemplation through art. A sceptic may wonder how, if there is no grandeur in the spectacle, there can be any in contemplating it. Having considered Wagner in some detail we must now turn to Tolstoy's criticism.

**Tolstoy on Wagner**

Tolstoy begins by considering Wagner's conception of drama. Drama, as Wagner conceives of it, both unites and transcends the various arts, transforming them into a total work, superior to what each could achieve in separation. Tolstoy's criticism, in effect, is that the unity to which Wagner refers is bogus; it is not organic but is imposed on the various arts through an exercise of the will. The various arts have a common material in human experience but each treats this material according to its own forms and values. For example, a great poem is already integrated. The attempt to integrate it further can only change it for the worse. A great poem may inspire a great song. But that does not mean the song in adding great music to the poem becomes greater than the poem taken by itself. Rather the music compensates for what in this setting is lost in the poem.

In short, where two arts are successfully combined, one takes a subordinate role. Thus a great opera is primarily a work in music. The words are subordinate. For rhythm is different in speech and in singing. The words in an opera can have the greatness of a play only by making the opera a great play with musical accompaniment. Thus integration, as Wagner conceives of it, is impossible. Greatness in art, as Tolstoy makes clear, is achieved only by respecting the values of some art in particular.

Having argued that Wagner's conception of drama is faulty, Tolstoy next considers how one is to account for his fame. He claims that Wagner's fame depends on his having exploited the devices of counterfeit art. Thus in a Wagnerian opera everything contributes to the illusion of originality and profundity. There is, first, a sense of the massive. Huge resources are involved in the very staging of a Wagnerian drama. The drama itself unfolds at immense length. The characters are not ordinary human beings but mythological figures, gods, dwarfs, giants, heroes. One is bewildered but also impressed; the drama seems to express in mythological form a profound philosophy of life. The philosophy is elusive but that adds to the impressiveness, for if it could easily be grasped it would not be profound. Meanwhile there are any number of striking and intriguing effects in the orchestra, including moments of genuine power and magnificence. Accompanying every performance, there is a barrage of publicity. Books, articles, manifestos pour forth defending the new art, attacking its critics and proclaiming its superiority to the art of all other times and places.

For Tolstoy this atmosphere of cloudy profundity is the mark of bogus art. Great art is characterized by lightness, clarity, simplicity and humanity. These qualities are lacking in the art of Wagner. To illustrate this, Tolstoy describes in some detail an actual performance of *The Ring*:

> When I arrived, an actor in jersey and tights was seated in front of an object intended to represent an anvil; his hair and beard were false; his hands, white and manicured, had nothing of the workman's; the carefree air, the bulging stomach, and the absence of muscle betrayed the actor. With an incredible hammer he struck as no one ever struck, a sword that was no less fanciful. It was easy to see he was a dwarf because he bent the knee as he walked. He shouted for a long time, his mouth strangely open ...[8]

It will be noted that Tolstoy is again using the so-called alienation effect. As in his first chapter, he is describing an opera, as it were, from the outside. The device is used throughout his description. The description is very amusing. But at this point a suspicion may occur to the reader. Might not any human activity be reduced to absurdity when it is described in this way? For described thus, its details appear at random so that we cannot see their relation to other details, nor therefore the relation of all those details to the point or sense of the whole. This is evident in the present case, because we know very well what Tolstoy is describing. For example, when he tells us that a man on the stage wears false hair and a false beard, he merely tells us that he is an actor. But we know that already. Precisely what we expect to see at a theatre are actors rather than real workmen, for real workmen, by and large, are not trained to act. There are of course many situations in life where a man wearing false hair and a false beard may appear ridiculous. But one of the situations where he will not appear ridiculous is when he appears on a stage.

In other words, Tolstoy in his description of Wagner's opera has fallen into an attitude hardly distinguishable from that of the philistine who objects to opera on the ground that people in real life do not communicate by singing. The classic response to that objection was given by Thomas De Quincey:

> In this argument lies an ignorance of the very first principle concerned in *every* Fine Art. In all alike, more or less directly, the object is to reproduce in the mind some great effect, through the agency of *idem in alio*. The *idem*, the same impression, is to be restored; but *in alio*, in a different material – by means of some different instrument. For instance, on the Roman stage there was an art, now entirely lost, of narrating, and in part of dramatically representing an impassioned tale, by means of dancing, of musical accompaniment in the orchestra and of elaborate pantomime in the performer ... Now suppose a man to object that young ladies, when saving their youthful husbands at midnight from assassination, could not be capable of waltzing or quadrilling, how wide is this of the whole problem! This is still seeking for the *mechanic* imitation, some imitation founded in the very fact; whereas the object is to seek the imitation in the sameness of the impression drawn from a different, or even from an impossible fact. If a man should say that he would 'whistle Waterloo', that is, by whistling connected with pantomime, would express the passion and the charge of Waterloo, it would be monstrous to refuse him his postulate on the pretence that people did not 'whistle at Waterloo'.[9]

The fault, then, of Tolstoy's chapter on Wagner is that he resorts to ridicule where he should have developed his criticism. This is a pity, for his criticism is very plausible. Wagner's conception of drama is certainly open to criticism. Moreover, in spite of his great talent, his influence on nineteenth-century music seems to me to have been a bad one. I think this can be demonstrated in relation to purely orchestral music, but let us confine ourselves to opera, which was his main concern.

The changes he introduced into opera are best appreciated by first looking at the main features of opera in the old style. The old opera was based on melodic writing for the voice. The main feature was the aria, which was delivered either in solo or in duet. Each aria would express a fresh melodic idea. Between the arias were the so-called recitatives. A recitative is delivered in something between singing and speaking; one might call it heightened speech. In the later nineteenth century, through Wagner's influence, this distinction between aria and recitative was ridiculed and treated as arbitrary. In fact it is not arbitrary but perfectly logical, for it is designed to give expression to the two sides of opera, music and drama. Thus the recitative was intended to further the drama or story; the aria was intended to express those elements in the story which were emotionally significant. The difference can easily be appreciated if one considers a non-musical drama. There will be remarks which are emotionally significant and others which are purely utilitarian. For example, if one character asks another to pass the salt, it is purely utilitarian. In opera that would be consigned to the recitative. By contrast, if one character tells another that he loves her, that is emotionally significant. In opera it would be expressed in an aria.

In the old opera, the orchestra was strictly subordinate to the voice, being used as accompaniment or support. This again was an object of criticism in the late nineteenth century. The older opera composers were ridiculed for the poverty of their orchestration. But the so-called poverty was deliberate. That is because the art was primarily vocal. As we shall see in a moment, it is impossible to give equal importance to voice and orchestra since the orchestra, where it does not obliterate, will divert attention from the voice.

Now, on Wagner's theory, opera must be integrated, equal importance being given to drama, voice and orchestra. The term music-drama was sometimes used to indicate the conception. A Wagnerian opera, in short, is intended to be not a display for the voice but a continuous drama in which the music is integrated into the action. To achieve this, Wagner virtually abolished the division between recitative and aria, the voice being used simply to further the drama. There are exceptions to this rule in his later operas but they are very few. For example, in *Die Valküre*, the second opera of *The Ring*, there is a passage for the tenor voice, made famous by Lauritz Melchior, which stands up as an aria. But one will have difficulty finding two or three others in the entire length of *The Ring*. At the same time as he abolished the division between recitative and aria, Wagner changed the status of the orchestra from that of accompaniment or support, giving it the role, hitherto confined to the aria, of expressing those elements in the drama which are emotionally significant. In achieving this, he used the so-called leitmotif. This is a short theme associated with some character, event or object in the drama. For example, the hero's sword will have a theme associated with it and this will strike up in the orchestra when the sword becomes important to the action. In this way, orchestra and drama are integrated, the orchestra continually reflecting what occurs on the stage.

In fact, however, as Tolstoy says, this appearance of integration is illusory. Wagner has merely reversed the order of subordination. In the old opera, the orchestra is subordinate to the voice; in Wagnerian opera, the voice is subordinate to the orchestra. For example, in obliterating the division between recitative and aria, Wagner in effect is confining the voice to continuous recitative. Its function, in short, is confined to the purely utilitarian. The orchestra becomes the dominant means of expression. Not only does Wagnerian opera fail as a mode of integration but it is also illogical. For precisely what makes opera distinctive is that it is based on the voice. The orchestra is already dominant in symphonic music. To make it dominant in opera also is not to supply a need but to obliterate an art. Saint-Saëns made the essential points in the 1880s:

> Formerly, people willingly forgot the drama to listen to the voices, and if the orchestra took it upon itself to be too engrossing there was complaint that it distracted attention.
>
> Nowadays, the public heeds the orchestra, trying to follow the myriad interwoven lines and the iridescent play of tone-colour. In so doing they forget to hear and see what is done upon the stage. The new system almost completely annihilates the art of singing, and boasts of this. Thus the sole *living* instrument, *the* instrument *par excellence*, is no longer entrusted with the rendering of melodic phrases. Other instruments, made by our hands in feeble imitation of the human voice, sing in its place. Is this not a handicap?[10]

It is worth remarking that the subordination of the voice has a harmful effect not simply on opera but indirectly on orchestral music also. The evidence for this may be taken from the writings of Wagner himself. As we have said, his writings come alive when he is discussing details of musical or theatrical performance. He has, for example, an interesting discussion of how a conductor should find the right tempo for a work. He says that many conductors cannot find the right tempo because they cannot *sing*. He means that they lack that inward relation to the melodic elements of a work which one acquires in singing, so that they impose on it a mechanical as opposed to a living tempo. He fails to mention, however, that this tendency was inherent in the development of the modern orchestra. Forces that vast can be held together only by having a tempo imposed on them by a conductor, as it were, from the outside. The subtleties of the vocal art are impossible in those circumstances. This will be appreciated by those who have listened to the recordings of singers trained within the Italian tradition, as it flourished in the nineteenth century. The recordings of the tenor Fernando de Lucia provide a good example. He exhibits a phenomenon one finds also in great poetry. His most striking effects are achieved, so to speak, against the basic metre which is never strictly followed, though always presupposed. Thus a note, or a pause, will be held to the point of disintegrating the rhythm as a whole but will at that point be released to preserve it. Then there are extraordinary changes in dynamics. The voice is taken from a mere thread of sound up to full power, or taken the other way, the full voice being drained of power and returned to a thread of sound. The effects are always, or so it seems, along a line, being reinforced by what has preceded them. The louder sounds acquire more power against the background of the soft, the soft appear even more so against the background of the loud. Moreover, the effects are not of mere display, or rarely so. In art this subtle, the slightest change in dynamics can carry an enormous emotional power. As Tolstoy says, art lies in the tiny details.

But the vocal art can achieve extraordinary subtlety only where the vocalist is not under the domination of a conductor or a composer. The position of the singer in Wagnerian opera is well illustrated by Wagner's article on Ludwig Schnorr, the tenor who created the role of Tristan. Schnorr died shortly after the performance and Wagner's article is intended as a tribute to his art. But his art seems to consist largely in his receptiveness to Wagner's instructions. He pictures the two of them in rehearsal; he is standing immediately to the side of Schnorr, whispering instructions into his ear as he sings. He is oblivious to the uncanny nature of the relation. It is that of a ventriloquist with his dummy.

It is a fact of history that Wagner did not create the opera of the future. For there has been no living tradition of Wagnerian opera. The only tradition consists in performing the operas of Wagner himself. Opera continued to flourish into the twentieth century. But the credit is due to composers in the Italian tradition, especially Verdi and Puccini. Moreover these composers not only enabled opera to flourish but also achieved the only genuine integration of its elements. Its elements are genuinely integrated not by giving them all an equal value, but by enriching each at its proper level of subordination. Thus the Italian composers of the late nineteenth century avoided a sharp contrast between recitative and aria and enriched their orchestration, while preserving the central importance of the vocal line. These developments are evident in the work of Puccini, a lesser composer than Verdi but one with a genius for the theatre. The first act of his *La Bohème*, for example, is a masterpiece of integration. The orchestra is handled in a symphonic style. The action is continuous, there being no sharp contrast between recitative and aria. But Puccini achieved this by shading the one into the other, not by abolishing the division. Thus the act ends in a conventional way, with two solo arias and a duet. But each solo begins at a conversational level, so that the whole aria emerges naturally from the preceding recitative. Above all, throughout the act, the writing for the voice is melodic and expressive. The Italian composers preserved the operatic tradition, because they were craftsmen as well as artists, who respected the forms of their art and whose aim was to communicate with their public, not to dominate it.

The Italian tradition came to an end in the twentieth century but the causes were external, not internal to the art. Italian audiences turned from opera to the cinema. When the Italian tradition ended, so, as a living tradition, did opera. Operas are still performed but the repertoire, so far as it has an audience, is taken from works composed in the nineteenth century. One may check this by reading Bernard Shaw's reviews of the seasons at Covent Garden in the 1890s.[11] The works he reviewed were those of his contemporaries. For example, he reviewed Bizet's *Carmen*, Mascagni's *Cavalleria Rusticana*, Leonardo's *I Pagliacci* and Puccini's *Tosca*. These are exactly the works which are likely to appear in a modern opera house, one hundred years later.

But the force of Tolstoy's criticism is best exhibited by turning to the content rather than the form of Wagner's art. Cloudy profundity, the affectation of sublimity without its substance, was what Tolstoy hated both in art and in life. For him the purity and beauty of Christianity for example, as found in the

Gospels, were obscured by the apparently profound but meaningless dogmas of the Church, by its incense, gorgeous costumes and elaborate ritual. Wagner he saw as providing a secular equivalent.

It will be useful here to consider Wagner's most remarkable work, *Tristan and Isolde*. It is based on a legend, allegedly of Celtic origin. In the first act, Tristan is escorting Isolde to Cornwall, where she is to wed King Mark. Tristan has killed the man to whom she was betrothed but she has fallen in love with him. He refuses to speak to her, out of respect for Mark, his king. In her resentment she contrives that they shall both drink a death potion. Her maid substitutes a love potion for the one intended. On drinking this, they openly declare their love for one another. In the second act, their love is consummated. This act is famous for its expression of erotic passion, perhaps the most uninhibited in the whole of art. Their relationship is discovered by a servant of the king, who is now her husband. Tristan is fatally wounded. In the last act, Tristan lies dying, in his castle in Brittany, where he has been taken for refuge. Isolde finds him and he dies in her arms. In the final scene, to music expressive of ecstatic consummation, she joins him in death.

The legend on which Wagner's opera is based traces the tragic consequences of ungovernable passion. The lovers are heedless of the order on which human life depends, cannot be restored to that order, and are therefore delivered over to the fatal consequences of their passion. But in Wagner's opera that theme is entirely transformed. His work makes continual play with a contrast between light and darkness. Light represents the natural order, social duty or obligation. Darkness represents the passion of Tristan and Isolde. It is clear that darkness is supposed to *transcend* light. In short, in their passion they have risen above the duties of ordinary life. Moreover, their love does not require as its basis that each should respect and value the other as a separate person. Rather it is a drive frustrated in its essence by that very separation. As a consequence, it can find its fulfilment only in death. In Wagner's opera, the death of Tristan and Isolde is not a punishment inherent in the workings of their passion; it is the very consummation of that passion. Their love, in some sense, is a love of death.

It may be noted that the love expressed in *Tristan and Isolde* is somewhat puzzling in its character. One may be inclined to suppose, indeed, that what Wagner seeks to express is not love but its perversion. The love of Tristan and Isolde, one may suppose, having lost its purity, has become on the part of each a mere drive to possess the other, this being so unbridled that only death can serve as their merciful release. But that interpretation cannot be correct, for, as we have seen, their love is supposed to lie not below but *above* the level of ordinary love. Indeed, it is supposed to transcend ordinary love even at its finest. The difficulty is to discover what exactly it is supposed to be.

We have seen that Wagner in the 1850s became influenced by the philosophy of Schopenhauer. Bryan Magee has suggested, perhaps correctly, that it is only in the light of Schopenhauer's philosophy that one can make overall sense of

Wagner's drama.[12] As we have seen, Wagner under the influence of Schopenhauer came to believe that the truth about life can be discovered not in action but only through the contemplation that is vouchsafed to a few gifted individuals. Through this contemplation those individuals discover the futility of life in all its striving. Central also in Schopenhauer's philosophy is the distinction between the phenomenal and the noumenal. The phenomenal is the world as it appears to the senses; the noumenal is ultimate reality which transcends the world. Plurality, the division of the world into particular objects, is a feature strictly of the phenomenal. At death, for example, separate individuality is dissolved into the noumenal. Now one may make some sense of Wagner's drama by supposing that Tristan and Isolde, being exceptional individuals, have had these truths revealed to them through their love. It has been revealed to them that life is futile and that death is their release and they have been able to anticipate that on obtaining this release they will be dissolved into the noumenal.

But there are a number of reasons why this interpretation, though it may make some sense of Wagner's drama, will certainly not explain its success. The first is that it has always been considered a weakness in a work of art that it should depend on a philosophy such as Schopenhauer's, undoubtedly controversial and hardly to be understood unless it is pondered independently of the work itself. The second is that whilst the interpretation may be correct, it is not at all likely to receive the unanimous approval of Wagnerians in general. It is noticeable, indeed, that Wagnerians, though they unanimously affirm the greatness of *Tristan and Isolde*, are by no means unanimous about what it seeks to communicate. Any given Wagnerian may provide a confident explanation but it is likely to differ from that provided by any other. The truth is that Wagner's art does not depend for its effectiveness on its central conceptions being scrutinized by the full intelligence. Its effectiveness depends rather on their *not* being so scrutinized.

To make this clear, let us return for a moment to the essentials of Tolstoy's own account of art. He has emphasized that art involves a variety of elements which may be separated in a partial analysis but which must be taken together in a final assessment. What is impressive on a partial analysis, for example, still waits for its final assessment on our having grasped the total conception of the work. Thus in great art reason cannot be kept separate from feeling, for the two are interfused. Feeling is purified by an exercise of the mind and intensified by the purification. We may take in illustration a great tragedy, such as Shakespeare's *Macbeth*. The central character in the drama, at a certain point, suffers a derangement of his senses and eventually enters into a state where life for him is entirely devoid of meaning. Now Shakespeare, at these points, is not seeking to induce in his audience comparable states of consciousness, thereby affording them, if only temporarily, unusual emotional experiences. The significance of the states can be grasped only where the intelligence is active upon the theme of the play. Moreover, the person whose intelligence is not active will be incapable of the proper *emotional* reaction to the play as a whole.

Now Wagnerian art works according to an opposing principle. For example, the extreme violence of expression in the second act of *Tristan and Isolde* is intended to induce in its audience the excitement that attends on the vicarious participation in extreme passion. The excitement is the aim. The aim of the drama as a whole is to keep the excitement going; or, rather, for the flesh is weak, even in the most fervent Wagnerian, to keep the audience in anticipation of future excitement. The feeling of profundity, it is true, is also essential to the Wagnerian art. But it is the *feeling* of profundity that is essential, not its substance. It is sufficient that the audience should have a sense of participating in states of consciousness stranger and more profound than any they could otherwise experience. Too close a scrutiny of those states would ruin the drama by dissipating the sense of profundity. Wagnerian art, in short, works in the manner of a drug. The aim is not that one should purify sensation through an exercise of mind but that one should lose one's mind in a flood of sensation.

Wagner has been worth considering in detail not simply because he served for Tolstoy as a paradigm of the counterfeit artist but because his influence was enormous on the decadent art of the late nineteenth and early twentieth centuries. The influence extended well beyond music. The attempt to evoke abnormal states of consciousness was common to many of the arts. For example, Arthur Rimbaud, a poet of great talent, practised a systematic derangement of his senses, through the use of drugs and by participating in experiences which were in conflict with the ordinary moral consciousness, in order to evoke in himself abnormal states which he could express in his poetry. He had the intelligence, before he was twenty, to abandon these practices. Others were not so fortunate. Hart Crane, a poet of comparable gifts, took his own life when he was in his early thirties. Yvor Winters, a friend of his, believed that there was a connection between his death and beliefs expressed in his poetry. He gives as an instance *The Dance*,

> where the language and feeling traditionally associated with love and the conviction of immortality appear to be applied to the experience of personal annihilation, so that the logical meaning of nearly every term at the crux of the poem is wholly at odds with the feelings implied. This seems to me a serious matter and probably has some relationship, at least, to the manner of Crane's end.[13]

A sense of this poisonous atmosphere will enable us to appreciate the greatness of Tolstoy's later work. It was Tolstoy, as Jacques Barzun said, who showed in his later work, in the midst of a contrary minded civilization, how great art could be achieved in unaffected simplicity.[14]

## Notes

1. A. Goldman and E. Sprinchorn, *Wagner on Music and Drama*, London, Gollancz, 1970, p. 11.
2. Ibid., p. 11 passim.
3. Quoted in Berlin, *The Roots of Romanticism*, pp. 95–6.
4. J. G. Fichte, *Addresses to the German Nation*, Chicago, Open Court, 1922. For a good account of these addresses see R. Adamson, *Fichte*, Edinburgh, Blackwood, 1881, pp. 84–92.
5. Berlin, *The Roots of Romanticism*, p. 96.
6. Goldman and Sprinchorn, *Wagner on Music and Drama*, pp. 60–61.
7. For an excellent account of Schopenhauer's views, see B. Magee, *The Philosophy of Schopenhauer*, Oxford, OUP, 1997.
8. *What is Art?*, p. 207.
9. Quoted in *The Pleasures of Music*, ed. J. Barzun, London, Michael Joseph, 1954, pp. 164–5.
10. Ibid., p. 226.
11. See Shaw, *Shaw's Music: The Complete Musical Criticism of Bernard Shaw, Volume 3: 1893–1950*, London, Bodley Head, 1981.
12. Magee, *The Philosophy of Schopenhauer*, pp. 350–402.
13. Ivor Winters, *Uncollected Essays and Reviews*, London, Allen Lane, 1974, pp. 141–2.
14. J. Barzun, *Darwin, Marx and Wagner*, Chicago, Chicago University Press, 1981, p. 311.

CHAPTER NINE

# Summary and Elaboration

We have now expressed the main points in Tolstoy's view of art. It is time to take stock. Tolstoy himself assists us in doing so, for in his fifteenth and sixteenth chapters he repeats and elaborates the main features of his account. Let us follow what he says.

He proceeds by distinguishing between the expressive quality in a work of art and its subject matter, what it expresses. He turns to the subject matter of art in his sixteenth chapter. He begins, in his fifteenth, with what is essential to genuine art, irrespective of subject matter. I have already suggested that we must not be misled by this procedure. Tolstoy does not mean that form and content are radically separate and can be assessed quite independently of each other. It is obvious, for example, that one cannot judge a writer's expression without having some idea of what he seeks to express. What Tolstoy means is that form and content are distinguishable aspects which must be held together in a final assessment but which can be separated for the purpose of analysis.

Setting aside subject matter, then, we find that the essential mark of genuine art is its infectiousness. A work is infectious when it recreates for its audience what its author has experienced or imagined. We may remember here the boy who related his experience on encountering a wolf. The boy's experience was recreated in that his words did not simply inform us of what occurred to him but enabled us to enter into it. We had the feeling of being there ourselves.

Infectiousness is indicative not simply of what is genuine in art but also of its importance. So far as one enters the boy's experience, one enters a viewpoint other than one's own. But art throws light on our own experience as well as that of others. We may recall the expression on Anna's face which Vronsky noticed in her portrait. The expression hardly fell outside his experience since he had often seen it. But what he had seen he did not really notice until it was recreated for him in art. Art throws light on our own experience because we now view it in an impersonal medium. We see in ourselves what others see but which they might not have told us or which we might not have heard since we would not have been listening. The experience is roughly comparable with that of hearing for the first time a recording of our own voice, which we have heard all our life, but from inside our own head. What emerges in the recording is our voice as others hear it. Thus through the experience of art we may learn both about others and about ourselves; in short, we may learn about life.

Tolstoy now states three conditions on which the infectiousness of a work depends: (*a*) the individuality of the feeling transmitted; (*b*) the clarity of its expression; and (*c*) the sincerity of the artist.

By the individuality of a feeling, Tolstoy means what is fresh or new about it. It is not the thought or feeling of which we are already fully aware but what we otherwise would not have noticed or considered that strikes and holds us in a work of art. By clarity of expression, he means expression fully realized. The work of an artist lies not simply in noticing what is fresh or new but precisely in expressing it, in bringing it home clearly both to the audience and to himself.

Sincerity needs to be considered in more detail. Tolstoy says it is the main consideration, the one on which the others depend. For if we detect insincerity in an author, he immediately loses us. We cannot be expected to enter into the viewpoint of an author who offers us one he cannot seriously enter into himself. Thus stated, Tolstoy's view may seem a matter of common sense. Indeed, that I believe is what we shall find it. Nevertheless it has been much criticized. The standard criticism is that Tolstoy is introducing psychological considerations which are independent of the author's text. We have the text but we do not know the author, nor therefore what passes through his mind in producing it. Take as an instance Shakespeare's *Macbeth*. Its theme is the corruption of power. We believe in seeing or reading the play that the corruption is real and that Shakespeare feels it to be so. But how can we know what he felt? We have the play but Shakespeare is unknown to us. How then can we judge whether he was sincere in producing it?

This criticism, it may be noted, presupposes that a work of art is not itself an intentional object, but rather one connected only contingently with intentions which may or may not pass through the author's mind but which in any case are essentially inaccessible to us. In that case, however, what difference would it make if we did know the author? Suppose Shakespeare were our contemporary. We ask him whether he was sincere in writing *Macbeth*. He tells us he was. But why should that settle the matter? If we cannot trust what he writes, why should we trust what he says? If what he writes are simply marks connected only contingently with his intentions, so are the words he utters. We have merely exchanged marks for sounds, and a person's intentions are as inaccessible in this case as in the other. Thus the view we are considering, consistently maintained, would make it impossible to detect sincerity in life as well as in art. In short, it would make it impossible as such to detect sincerity.

Perhaps there are those who are inclined to accept this sceptical conclusion, in which case, they would be well advised to consider their assumptions. Reflection will reveal that they are working with an incoherent idea of the mental. To illustrate the point, let us switch from the author to the reader. We may read a work either aloud or silently. If we read silently, we read 'in the mind'. Now there are those who suppose that what is 'in the mind', in the sense just indicated, is co-extensive with the mental. For example, even when we read aloud – or so it is supposed – we are essentially reading 'in the mind', the sounds we utter being mere physical accompaniment. It is this idea which leads to scepticism. The mental is identical with what is 'in the mind'. What is 'in the mind' is essentially private; so, therefore is the mental. It follows that we can never detect another's mental processes.

To see the incoherence of this view, we have only to recall what we already know. It is obvious, for example, that reading 'in the mind' is a later accomplishment. Everyone learns to read by reading aloud. The view we are considering has reversed the real order of dependence. Reading 'in the mind' is in fact a later refinement, which is possible only because we have first read aloud. Indeed silent reading is a late accomplishment in the history of reading itself. For centuries all reading was aloud. It follows that the mental cannot be reduced to what is 'in the mind'. Reading aloud as much as reading 'in the mind' is a mental activity. But it is a mental activity which involves the mastery of spoken sounds and is exhibited, therefore, in the use of those sounds, not in some other activity occurring in private. Were it otherwise, no child would ever learn to read.

Now similarly, Shakespeare's intentions are grasped in his use of words. We follow his words because, in the marks he has written, we grasp what he means and therefore what he intends. It is true that we can be deceived. An author whom we take to believe in what he writes may be manipulating us. But that in itself is no cause for scepticism, for it allows, indeed presupposes, that often we are not deceived. We can envisage being deceived in this case, because we know the difference between sincerity and insincerity and in general, therefore, can distinguish between the two. The sceptical view is quite different. It supposes that since we lack direct access to the author's private mental processes, we can *never* know what he intends. But this is incoherent since if it were impossible to tell an author's intentions from what he writes, it would be equally impossible to tell by direct access to his private mental processes. To see this, we have only to reconsider the case of reading. As we have seen, 'reading in the mind' is only to do silently what we have been taught to do aloud. But then if it were impossible to tell that a person can read from what he does aloud, it would be equally impossible to tell by direct access to what he does silently 'in the mind'. This must be so, since there is nothing he can do silently which he could not have done aloud.

We return, then, to common sense. As Tolstoy says, we do not take seriously an artist who is not sincere, who does not believe in what he seeks to express. It is true that art is not always serious. There is room in art for pure fantasy or make-believe. But we shall not concentrate on those cases if we wish to bring out what is important in art. We shall concentrate rather on those elements in art which make for greatness. Now there would be no greatness in art unless there were artists who do believe in what they seek to express and in the value of expressing it. In short, there would be no greatness in art unless there were artists who do take their work seriously.[1]

Tolstoy, then, setting aside subject matter, sees the importance of art as lying in its infectiousness. That is because there can be no importance in art unless there is a connection between art and life. Art is connected with life precisely where it is infectious. As we have said, art is infectious where it recreates or expresses life as it is experienced by its authors. Thus art and life are connected precisely through the ability of the one to recreate or express the other.

Before turning to what Tolstoy says about the subject matter of art, it will be useful to consider in more detail what is involved in the expressive relation between art and life. Tolstoy concentrates, as we have seen, on the expression of feeling or emotion. For this he has been criticized.[2] It has been said, for example, that not all art is expressive in the way he claims. Thus within music we may distinguish between the expressive and the non-expressive without necessarily criticizing the latter. Only some music is naturally described as expressing emotion. The same point applies to painting, which may be abstract as well as representational. Expressiveness therefore cannot serve as a definition of art. The point is true as it stands, but as we shall see in a moment, Tolstoy is not attempting to define art. His aim is to indicate its objective features, its grounds, characteristics and consequences. In this he is guided by the problem he sets himself in his first chapter. As he there makes clear, his problem is to show what is important about art, to show (given the labour and expense involved) what justifies it.

Now unlike a craft such as plumbing, literature or any comparable art does not cater to a need which is immediate or practical. In this it resembles an art of amusement which produces objects amusing or pleasurable in themselves. But we sense also a difference in that it seems to offer us something more important than amusement. The products of such an art offer us an interest which is at once an interest in themselves and an interest in life, so that we may increase our understanding of life by increasing our understanding of such an art. But that would be impossible unless within the art there were an intimate connection with life. As Tolstoy says, the connection in such an art lies in its expressiveness. We may rephrase exactly the same point. Remove from art its expressive qualities. You will not remove the whole of art, but you will certainly remove the greatest. Wherever there is greatness or profundity in art there is that recreation of life which we may term expressiveness. That is precisely why Tolstoy concentrates on the expressiveness of art.

There are, however, difficulties in making clear the expressive relation in art, and it will be useful if we now attend to them. In the main, these difficulties are analogous to those involved in making clear the relation between intention and act. As we have seen, there is a tendency to treat an act as connected only contingently with its intention, which is essentially private. The relation between an emotion and its expression is often treated in the same fashion. Thus the emotion is treated as being 'in the mind', in short essentially private, and its expression as mere physical accompaniment.

However, an emotion is no more essentially 'in the mind' than is an intention. An angry child, for example, gets red in the face, screams and kicks the furniture. Gradually he may acquire a sense that in this behaviour he is making himself obnoxious to others and may attempt to control it. Eventually he may succeed on many occasions in completely hiding his anger. His anger now exists, we may say, independently of physical expression, entirely 'in the mind'. It does not follow that it was always 'in the mind', even when he was a child, so that its physical expression even at that time was mere accompaniment. That would be to confuse a later accomplishment with the primary phenomenon. The fallacy is comparable, we may note, with the one we encountered in the case of reading. There, a later accomplishment, silent reading, is treated as more fundamental than the primary phenomenon, reading aloud. Here the later accomplishment, silent anger, is treated as more fundamental than the primary phenomenon, anger embodied.

If we reflect, we shall find that an emotion involves the whole person, in thought, feeling and act. In short, it has many sides. Not every side need be present on any given occasion. Yet no side is more essential than any other. The point is important for our purpose since the expressive relation in art depends on emotion in its embodied form. As Tolstoy said, art depends on natural expressions of emotion. We smile when happy; weep when sad. These expressions are in a manner infectious. Through them we share in one another's happiness or grief. Art arises through an elaboration of these expressions.

We may take a simple example in illustration. In a few lines one can sketch a sad or happy face. We call it sad or happy because it copies the facial expressions of people who are sad or happy in real life. For example, in the drawing of a happy face, the line representing the mouth will turn up at its ends, resembling the way the mouth turns up at the corners when we grin. In the drawing of a sad face, the line will turn down at its ends, as the mouth droops when we are sad. Where $A^1$ resembles A we tend to react to $A^1$ as we would to A. That is the principle at work in the present case. Through the resemblance between a face and the drawing we apply the same word to the drawing as we would to the face. Artistic resemblance, of course, is not identical with artistic representation. We must take into account also the line of intention. Thus we make a drawing with the intention of its resembling a face, not a face with the intention of its resembling a drawing. That is why it is not the face that represents the drawing but the drawing that represents the face. Nevertheless, representation commonly works through resemblance.

We may take a further example. New Orleans funerals were accompanied by a band, which played sad music on the way to the funeral; on the way back the music turned joyous signifying the return to life. We can find such music on record. If we walk in time with the music on the first part of the record we will find ourselves making slow and heavy movements as though burdened with sadness; to follow the music on the second part we will have to skip and jump as though in delight. In short, the rhythm of the music enacts the rhythm of those emotions. In that way it expresses them, infecting the listener first with sadness, then with joy.

The above account, however, has its critics. Roger Scruton in a recent work provides an example. He there denies that one can explain artistic representation or expressiveness by reference to resemblance. His argument is that art does not in fact resemble (or sufficiently resemble) life. 'The picture that Leonardo painted of the Mona Lisa,' he says, 'resembles a picture of a dog far more than it resembles a woman.'[3] In short, a picture will resemble any other picture more than it resembles life. Consequently there cannot be a resemblance between art and life which is sufficient to explain how the one can represent the other. This view, were it true, would certainly have remarkable consequences. For example, a child will resemble any other child more than it resembles its father. It follows, on Scruton's view, that there can be no significant resemblance between a father and his child. Scruton is plainly assuming, as De Quincey put it, that one cannot whistle Waterloo because at Waterloo no one whistled. In other words, he is assuming that a significant resemblance can hold only amongst similar objects. The significant resemblance is usually the one that holds among objects otherwise *dissimilar*. Thus, as De Quincey said, it is precisely the dissimilarities between art and life that gives significance to the resemblances between them. In art, life appears as in an unaccustomed context. Just for that reason resemblances with life strike home and hold the attention. In consequence we attend to features of life which in life itself we might not have noticed at all.

Tolstoy has now dealt with art on its expressive or infectious side. He next turns to its subject matter.

## The Subject Matter of Art

It is important to recall that in turning to the subject matter of art we are turning to what has already been implicit in our discussion of expressiveness. As we have said, we cannot judge an artist's expression unless we know what he seeks to express. We turn then to the subject matter of art not as to an element foreign to the expressive relation but in order to single out an aspect of that relation for our special attention.

To give point to Tolstoy's account, let us recall that we are a mixture of good and evil and that art may appeal to the evil in us as well as the good. Suppose, for example, that there is a story written in the spirit of hatred or contempt and we are drawn into it, sharing the emotions expressed. Perhaps it is a story, such as Maupassant's, about the seduction of a mother and her daughter. The apparent modesty of the women is revealed to be a sham. We feel a certain contempt for the women and are amused by the superiority of their seducers. Afterwards, however, the story leaves a bad taste in the mouth. The story, we may suppose, is skilful and evocative; it has infected us, drawn us in. Are we to say, therefore, that it is good aesthetically? The bad taste, perhaps, has a different source, namely, in our moral sense, which we later bring to bear on the subject matter of the story. Some would not only endorse that distinction but would argue that the moral judgement is based on grounds external to the story itself. Being an aesthetic object, the story should be judged on aesthetic or artistic ground. In short, we should be concerned, in judging the story, not with the subject matter but purely with its artistic treatment.

Let us note, however, that by the subject matter of the story we mean its events as related by the author. These are not external to the story but at its heart. The author's expression would not have moved us unless we had lent ourselves imaginatively to the events he related and to the attitude with which he related them. For example, a better person than ourselves would not have lent himself in that way. To him the story would not have been infectious and would therefore not have been successful on any ground, aesthetic or otherwise. What is certainly not true is that the author's expression will move us quite independently of any attitude we have towards the events he relates. It may move us independently of our moral attitudes but that is because we have given free rein to our non-moral or immoral ones.

If we reflect, we shall find that 'artistic judgement' is ambiguous. It may refer to the narrowly aesthetic. Getting the sense of a story, we may leave it presupposed and concentrate on the author's choice of words at this or that point. Here our judgement is artistic in the narrowly aesthetic sense. But by an artistic judgement we may mean a judgement of the work as a whole. Here the subject matter of the story cannot be irrelevant since it is integral to the work as a whole and that is what we are seeking to judge. To illustrate the point, consider the following passage by Evelyn Waugh. He is describing a school of art which was run by a Catholic priest for African boys:

> The boy's first task is always to make a mask which will 'frighten his little brother'. It is explained to him that it is far easier to make ugly things than beautiful; that, implicitly, the paintings of Mr Francis Bacon are a rudimentary accomplishment which the Mashona boy must outgrow. The highest achievement is to make something lovable, an image of angel or saint, of Our Lady or Our Lord, before which it is easy to pray. Before this stage is approached the use of the chisel is taught and the composition of ornaments that express a moral lesson or a theological tenet. Art is the catechism and prayer in visible form. There is no suggestion of self-expression or of aesthetic emotion; nor of acquiring a marketable skill or titillating national pride at doing as well as the white man.[4]

The criticism of Francis Bacon, in the above passage, concerns his choice of subject matter. But it concerns his subject matter as revealing an impoverishment in his *art*. The implication is that his preference for the shocking or horrific is really a preference for the easy over the difficult accomplishment. It is irrelevant whether or not we agree with Waugh's judgement. The point for our purpose is that his judgement, correct or incorrect, is an *artistic* one. It is well known, for example, in art quite generally, that good is harder to portray then evil. In literature the interesting characters are usually the bad ones. In part this is the result of the artistic medium. We have already noted as a strength in art that it stands at a certain distance from life. It is because of this distance that art enables us to notice features of life that otherwise we would have overlooked. But there is a price to pay for this virtue. In its distance from life art enables us to contemplate and enjoy what in real life we would neither enjoy nor even contemplate. The principle at work is the one we find in news broadcasting, where what is most readily available is the sensational and horrific. Even extreme depravity in these circumstances can be contemplated with interest. In this there is an evident falsification of life. In life it is extreme depravity which is of all things the most unbearable to contemplate; genuine goodness the freshest and most wonderful. Nevertheless, it is a falsification which flourishes in art of the second rank. Only a great master, such as Tolstoy himself, can give to goodness in art the body or substance which we find in real life. Now Bacon's art, if Waugh is correct, involves this falsification and is of the second rank. This criticism of Bacon is not narrowly aesthetic but it is certainly artistic, for it is aimed directly at his art.

Tolstoy's conception of art, as will be evident, is very similar to the one expressed by Waugh in the above passage. For both, the value of art is linked to its consequences or role in life. If it is to be a force for good, the goodness in it must be fostered and its corruptions criticized. This means a raising not a lowering of artistic standards. As we have said, the expression of goodness is the harder task, even in the narrowly aesthetic sense.

To support his point, Tolstoy repeats some of the material from earlier chapters. For example, he repeats his historical survey, in order to emphasize that where art has flourished in the past it has never had as its aim a narrowly aesthetic one but has sought to express beliefs or attitudes which are fundamental to its society. Here also we encounter, once more, Tolstoy's progressivism. As we have seen, he believes that since the Middle Ages Christianity has been undergoing a process of purification and that it is destined to flourish in its purest form. The art of the future therefore will give expression to a Christianity thus purified. It does not follow that it must be specifically religious. Tolstoy distinguishes between two types of art, the religious and the universal. Both types will flourish in the society he anticipates. Religious art will concern itself specifically with the love of God and of one's neighbour. Universal art will give expression to Christianity in a more indirect form. For Tolstoy, as we have seen, Christianity is pre-eminently the religion of a common humanity. Universal art will give expression to this theme by dealing with those attitudes, feelings or beliefs which are common to all human beings and which serve to unite them.

We must dwell for a while on what Tolstoy means by universal art, for it has been widely misunderstood. A common view is that he means an art that will appeal quite literally to everyone. This in effect is to say that art should appeal not simply to the unsophisticated but even to the ignorant. In effect, therefore, Tolstoy is advocating that we lower artistic standards in the interest of moral or religious views. Now that is entirely to misunderstand him. His 'universal' is normative, not statistical. He knew very well that art cannot appeal quite literally to everyone, whatever the circumstances. There are numerous passages to this effect in *What is Art?* He states explicitly, for example, that people who have become habituated to the art of his time may not simply fail to appreciate universal art, but may have become incapable of doing so. They may genuinely prefer the second-rate. Those, for example, who are habituated to Wagnerian orchestration will not readily appreciate the beauty of unadorned melody. They will find it insipid. One may compare them to the old drunkard who can no longer taste anything weaker than brandy. Nor by universal art does Tolstoy mean one that appeals to the simple as opposed to the learned, but rather one that will appeal to learned and simple alike.

Tolstoy's 'universal', then, is normative. Further, as we have already implied, the norms involved are those of *art*, not of a morality applied externally to the artistic process. His ideal is indistinguishable from that of classical art. The best art is universal in the sense that it transcends passing fashion and local significance and gives lasting expression to what is of permanent value in human life. It is evident that such an art cannot appeal quite literally to everyone. For example, there may be periods when people are wholly absorbed in what is of passing fashion or local significance. The best art is universal because it is addressed to people who are *not* so absorbed. In consequence its appeal is not limited to a given time or place but is available for indefinitely many people at innumerably different times and places. Tolstoy, it is true, believes that such an art in his own time is more likely to appeal to the simple than to the sophisticated but that is because he believes that the sophisticated in his time are absorbed in what is of passing fashion or local significance. They are divorced from what is universal in a way that simpler people – or so he believes – are not. We may illustrate these points by reference to Tolstoy's comments on the story of Joseph, one of his examples of universal art:

> The author of the novel of Joseph did not need to describe in detail, as would be done nowadays, the blood-stained coat of Joseph, the dwelling and dress of Jacob, the pose and attitude of Potiphar's wife, and how adjusting the bracelet on her left arm she said, 'Come to me', and so on, because the content of feeling in this novel is so strong that all details except the most essential – such as that Joseph went out into another room to weep – are superfluous and would only hinder the transmission of emotion. And therefore this novel is accessible to all men, touches people of all nations and classes young and old, and has lasted to our times and will yet last for thousands of years to come. But strip the best novels of our time of their details and what will remain?[5]

The story of Joseph is one of jealousy, betrayal, mercy and forgiveness. The themes are universal. The treatment is classical. Not a word is spared for atmosphere or local colour, thereby, as Tolstoy says, emphasizing the universality of the themes. There is some repetition but only of the kind that is integral to the telling of a story, especially when the story-teller has his audience before him. Otherwise there is not a superfluous detail. Nowhere do we get the impression that the story has been made interesting through the art of its author. The impression rather is that the story is so interesting in itself that he had only to tell it. On reflection we realize that this itself is supreme art. The story is ageless, one of the masterpieces of world literature. When Tolstoy spoke of universal art it was such a story that he had in mind as a model. One can hardly complain of his lowering artistic standards. It would be more plausible to complain of his pitching them too high.

Tolstoy does not suppose, however, that universal art must always be of major significance. He mentions, for example, that good art may be found in the art of ornamentation. He anticipates that the reader may think him inconsistent. Throughout *What is Art?* he has criticized those who explain art in terms of beauty and has emphasized its expressiveness. Ornaments are valued less often for their expressive qualities than for their beauty. He claims rightly, however, that the inconsistency is only apparent. The desire to surround oneself with objects that are a delight to the senses is a universal one. Beauty in this sense, therefore, is a legitimate object for universal art. Tolstoy's criticism is reserved for those who see beauty as the only significant feature in art and seek to explain the whole of art in terms of it.

There is little excuse, therefore, for supposing that Tolstoy's conception of art involves a lowering of artistic standards. So far as such an excuse may be found, it lies in Tolstoy's choice of examples to illustrate universal art. In his choice from the modern period, he is too often moved by his heart rather than his head and is inclined to see accomplishment where there is only good intention. The fault is especially evident in his discussion of painting, where in any case he is ill qualified to judge. Here he is quite reckless in judging works by their overt subject matter rather than by their subject matter as revealed in artistic treatment. For all that, his critics have no excuse for the emphasis they place on this fault. Tolstoy quite explicitly warns his readers that his examples may be faulty and urges them to concentrate on what he seeks to illustrate and not simply on the illustrations themselves.[6]

The real fault in Tolstoy's sixteenth chapter lies in his grasp of social conditions rather than in his grasp of art. He is too ready to assume that the conditions for great art are as available in the present as they have been in the past. In particular he underestimates the power of industrialization and its effect on traditional culture. The fault is especially evident in his concluding chapters. We may consider briefly his nineteenth, where he describes the art of the future. Here he anticipates a state of society in which commercial influences have entirely disappeared from art. The artist will earn his living not through his art but through common labour. In that way art will be produced not because the artist is forced to say something but only because he has something to say. The role of the artist in this society is evidently that of an artist in a traditional culture, Tolstoy having assumed not simply that this culture will be preserved but that it will become universal. The forces that tend to its destruction and give rise to decadent art are assumed simply to have disappeared through the influence of a purified Christianity.

At various points, in dealing with Tolstoy's account, we have referred implicitly to other and conflicting theories. It will be useful now if we consider the more important in some detail. We shall then be in a position to compare them more explicitly with Tolstoy's own.

## Notes

1 By serious, of course, I do not mean solemn. A work of comic inspiration may be as serious in the required sense as any tragedy.
2 See, for example, Wilkinson, 'Art, Emotion and Expression', pp. 234–5.
3 See R. Scruton, *The Aesthetics of Music*, Oxford, Clarendon Press, 1997, p. 122.
4 Evelyn Waugh, *A Tourist in Africa*, London, Methuen, 1960, pp. 128–9.
5 *What is Art?*, pp. 244–5.
6 See ibid., p. 246, p.1.

CHAPTER TEN

# Alternative Theories

Yvor Winters argued that the various theories of art are less numerous than one might suppose.[1] He classified them under four headings: the didactic, the hedonistic, the romantic and the moralistic. The last theory is very similar to Tolstoy's own. Let us therefore consider the other three.

The *didactic* theory holds that the value of art lies in its content, where this is distinguishable from its artistic treatment. This is a theory we have only to note, for we have already considered it in sufficient detail.

The *hedonistic* theory holds that the value of art lies in the pleasure or enjoyment it affords. The theory appears in various forms. Winters offers a criticism which applies to the theory in all its forms. It is worth quoting, for it expresses, with classic power, the objections Tolstoy himself had against defining art in terms of pleasure:

> The term *pleasure* is applied indiscriminately to widely varying experiences: we say, for example, that we derive pleasure from a glass of good whiskey and that we derive pleasure from reading *Hamlet*. The word is thus misleading, for it designates two experiences here which have little relationship to each other. There is a great range in the kinds of pleasure advocated in various hedonistic philosophies, but in general one might remark this defect which is common to nearly all, perhaps all, such systems: pleasure is treated as an end in itself, not as a by-product of something else. If we recognize that certain feelings which are loosely classifiable as forms of pleasure result from our recognition of various kinds of truth and from the proper functioning of our nature in the process of this recognition, we then have a principle which may enable us to distinguish these pleasures from pleasures less important or less desirable, such as the pleasures or satisfactions which we derive from the gratification of physical appetites or from the excitement of stimulants, and a principle which may even enable us to evaluate relatively to each other the higher pleasures themselves. But pleasure then becomes incidental and not primary, and our system can no longer be classified as properly hedonistic.[2]

We must pay special attention to one of the forms which the hedonistic theory assumes. In this form a sharp separation is made between artistic experience and all other experience:

> T. S. Eliot, for example, tells us that the human experience about which the poem appears to be written has been transmuted in the aesthetic process into something new which is different in kind from all other experience. The poem is not then, as it superficially appears, a statement about a human experience, but is a thing in itself ... The aim of the poem so conceived is

again pleasure, pleasure conceived as intensity of emotion; but the emotion is of an absolutely special sort.[3]

Winters is here describing what is known to us as the doctrine of art for art's sake. It is the doctrine to which Tolstoy is especially opposed. As we have seen, it reverses the didactic theory. The value of art lies not in its content but precisely in its artistic treatment. The doctrine is linked to the hedonistic theory in that artistic treatment is supposed to offer a pleasure peculiar to itself, the pleasure of aesthetic form. The writers most commonly associated with the doctrine, at least in Britain, are Oscar Wilde and Clive Bell. We shall soon consider them in some detail.

Both the didactic and the hedonistic theories explain art by relating it, though in different ways, to its audience. The *romantic* theory places its emphasis on the artist. According to this theory, communication is a secondary or even an incidental end in art. Art is primarily self-expression. Thus the aim of a true artist in creating his work is not to cater to an audience. He is wholly occupied with expressing in his chosen medium his own thoughts or feelings. The theory had its origin in the Romantic movement of the nineteenth century. But we shall be considering it in a more recent version.

We have isolated for our attention the doctrine of art for art's sake and the romantic theory. Let us begin with the former.

**Art for Art's Sake**

This doctrine was expressed in its most sophisticated form by the critics Clive Bell and Roger Fry. But it was given its wittiest expression by Oscar Wilde, to whom Tolstoy himself refers. Wilde's aesthetic views are scattered through his critical writings.[4] He was primarily a humorist, and exaggeration for comic effect was one of his main devices. Nevertheless a fairly clear aesthetic emerges, one which was later elaborated by others into a philosophy. Its best-known expression is in Wilde's preface to *The Picture of Dorian Gray*:

> The artist is the creator of beautiful things.
> There is no such thing as a moral or an immoral book. Books are well written or badly written. That is all.
> No artist has ethical sympathies. An ethical sympathy in an artist is an unpardonable mannerism of style.
> We can forgive a man for making a useful thing as long as he does not admire it. The only excuse for making a useless thing is that one admires it intensely.
> All art is quite useless.[5]

Art is useless, on Wilde's view, because it does not belong to the sphere of the practical. Its aim is to adorn life, not to advance it. It is essentially artificial, made up, contrived. Its chief aim is to give pleasure. But the supreme pleasure is the pleasure in art itself. What interests the artist is not his subject matter but its artistic treatment. In great art, the artistic treatment achieves or approximates to perfect beauty. The moral is a category distinct from the aesthetic. It may enter into the subject matter of art. But it is the artistic treatment that is important in art, not its subject matter. Thus art can be assessed only in aesthetic terms.

There are other remarks in Wilde's preface which are worth considering. For example, 'From the point of view of form, the type of all the arts is the art of the musician. From the point of view of feeling, the actor's craft is the type.' If an actor has to portray nobility of character, we judge him as an actor by whether he portrays it on the stage not by whether he exhibits it in life. If he exhibits it in life but cannot portray it on the stage, he may be a good man but he is a bad actor. The aim of the actor, one might say, is to portray the *form* of nobility. Whether he has its substance is irrelevant. For that reason the type of all the arts is that of the musician. For music is the least representational of the arts. One judges it by its forms, not by what it represents. Or, again, 'All art is at once surface and symbol. Those who go beneath the surface do so at their peril. Those who read the symbol do so at their peril.' There is a common tendency to suppose that the meaning of a work lies in something not portrayed in the work itself, so that to find its meaning one needs, as it were, to dig beneath its surface. A famous psycho-analytic study of *Hamlet*, for example, claimed that the real meaning of the work lies in Shakespeare's relations to his mother and father. Wilde, by contrast, argues that one needs to look further along the surface. In other words, it is the work as a whole that provides the key to its symbols. If you wish to know what is symbolized at one point in a play, see how it is connected with the play at other points. In that sense, a work of art is all surface. *Hamlet*, for example, exists only in the form in which Shakespeare created it.

*The Picture of Dorian Gray* was condemned by some leading journals as immoral. Wilde leaped to its defence, sending numerous letters to the journals concerned. This is normally a serious error. Writers are ill advised to respond in public to criticism of their work since the public, assuming they are biased, will sympathize with their opponents. Wilde, however, was an exception to that rule. His letters are so amusing that one sympathizes not with his opponents but with him. The theme of his letters is that the charge of immorality is irrelevant, since morality has nothing to do with art:

> Your reviewer suggests that I do not make it sufficiently clear whether I prefer virtue to wickedness or wickedness to virtue. An artist, sir, has no ethical sympathies at all. Virtue and wickedness are to him simply what the colours on his palette are to the painter. They are no more and they are no less. He sees that by their means a certain artistic effect can be produced, and he produces it. Iago may be morally horrible and Imogen stainlessly pure. Shakespeare, as Keats said, had as much delight in creating the one as he had in creating the other.[6]

Oscar Wilde's value for us is representative. He gave witty expression to views which were fashionable among artists in the late nineteenth century and to which Tolstoy was directly opposed. The reader may already have noticed, however, that Wilde's remarks depend for their force on his exposing weaknesses in the didactic theory and in that sense are parasitic upon it. A good example is his remark that the meaning of a symbol in art lies on its surface. The remark has force in emphasizing the importance of artistic form and in exposing those who search for irrelevant connections between art and life. Further attention to his remarks reveals, however, that he has simply reversed the didactic theory. The didacticist emphasizes life at the expense of those elements that are distinctive of art. Wilde emphasizes the artistic elements at the expense of life. That there is a dichotomy between the two is common to both the parties. It is a significant feature of Tolstoy's account that he rejects the dichotomy.

To clarify the point, let us consider how the doctrine of art for art's sake was developed by later theorists. Wilde was concerned primarily with literature but the doctrine had its greatest influence on the visual arts. It was developed in particular by the art critics Clive Bell and Roger Fry. These critics were enthusiastic in supporting the work of leading French artists such as Cézanne, Van Gogh and Gauguin. They called these artists Post-Impressionists and helped to make their work known in Britain. The term Post-Impressionist was meant to indicate that the work of these artists constituted an advance on Impressionism. As we have seen, the Impressionist painters, who specialized in effects of light, were not at first appreciated. People were puzzled by the lack of firm outline in their paintings. However, a lack of outline is a characteristic effect of light. In strong light or extreme heat, for example, objects begin to shimmer and lose their outline. By the turn of the century, people had become accustomed to the Impressionists and their work was well appreciated. At that point, artists began to search for different styles. Impressionism, in any case, is inherently limited. The painter who concentrates on effects of lights must thereby neglect other aspects of nature, such as its mass or solidity. It was precisely the effect of mass on solidity that Cézanne, especially in his later work, attempted to capture. Other artists attempted other effects. Van Gogh's landscapes, for example, seem to embody violent emotion.

So far, the issues raised may seem artistic rather than philosophical. What we have described is a change in artistic style. A change in artistic style is hardly an occasion for surprise. Nature is, after all, infinitely various. No artistic style can exhaust her. Indeed, in that sense every artistic style is inherently limited. For example, if, like Cézanne, you concentrate on effects of solidity or mass, you cannot, like the Impressionists, concentrate on subtle effects of light. Bell and Fry, however, saw the matter differently. Bell, in particular, thought that Cézanne's work constituted an advance not simply in the sense of stimulating a fresh interest but in the sense of expressing, more profoundly than ever before, the quality essential to all art. The quality essential to all art he called significant form.

Bell explains what he means by significant form in *Art*, his main work in aesthetic theory. He begins by saying that aesthetic theory requires a combination of sensibility and rigorous thought. Thus one cannot develop an aesthetic theory unless one has a grasp in practice of what art is, and this requires the sensibility to respond to particular works. But in addition one requires rigorous thought in order to arrive at a theory of what one responds to in the particular case. In Bell's view, an aesthetic theory will take the form of specifying what all works of art have in common:

> For either all works of art have some common quality, or when we speak of 'works of art' we gibber. Everyone speaks of 'art', making a mental classification by which he distinguishes the class 'works of art' from all other classes. What is the justification of this classification? What is the quality common and peculiar to all members of this class?[7]

In order to isolate the quality he is seeking, Bell looks first at an example of pseudo art. If we can find what is lacking in pseudo art, we shall find also what is essential to genuine art. He takes as his example a famous Victorian painting, *Paddington Station*. The artist, Frith, has taken a typical scene at a well-known railway station and represented it in realistic detail. Bell acknowledges not only that the work is well done but also that it is interesting and amusing. Nevertheless he denies that it is a work of art:

> *Paddington Station* is not a work of art; it is an interesting and amusing document. In it line and colour are used to recount anecdotes, suggest ideas, and indicate the manners and customs of an age: they are not used to provoke aesthetic emotions. Forms and relations of forms were for Frith not objects of emotion, but means of suggesting emotion and conveying ideas.[8]

Frith is not a real artist, because he uses line and colour to express something about life. For the real artist line and colour are of interest in themselves. In Bell's terms, the real artist is interested in *significant form*. For him, line and colour are themselves objects of emotion. But this emotion is purely aesthetic, because it has as its object only the formal or aesthetic qualities of art. The connection of this view with Wilde's will be evident.

For Bell, then, the quality essential to all real art is significant form. He proceeds to justify this view by arguing, for example, that a painting such as *Paddington Station* has been rendered pointless by the development of photography. The camera can represent the world as well as an artist. But photography is not art. It follows that the concern of real art cannot be to represent the world. It is concerned, rather, with significant form.

Bell's work is a pre-eminent example of the influence of aesthetic theory on artistic practice. His views of course are not original. As we have seen, they were common property among many artists in the nineteenth century. But by giving them a theoretical form he strengthened their influence. During the 1920s art became increasingly abstract, this tendency culminating in the 1950s, when representational content disappeared almost entirely from the visual arts. Strictly speaking, that consequence did not follow directly from Bell's theory. He did not claim that real art invariably dispenses with representational content. That claim would have lacked all plausibility. The whole of European art, before the twentieth century, is representational. His claim, rather, was that where art has representational content, it is not this content that gives it artistic value. For example, the artistic value of a portrait by Rembrandt does not depend, as one might at first have thought, on what it reveals about human character. Character is merely an occasion for a composition in line and colour. It is through its compositional power rather than through its content that Rembrandt's portrait has value. Still, though Bell's theory did not strictly entail, it certainly encouraged, the drive towards abstraction. For if the representational content of art is not of artistic value there is no necessity to include it, and then it is a short step to leaving it out altogether.

As we have said, Bell's work exhibits the influence of aesthetic theory on artistic practice. But it exhibits also the danger of such an influence. The reader may already have noted the weakness in his account. He is involved in at least two fallacious assumptions, these being not incidental but essential to his theory. For example, he begins by stating that there is a quality common to all art. This view is essential to his theory. It will be idle to specify significant form as the quality all works of art have in common, if all works of art have no quality in common. Bell's argument to show that all works of art must have such a quality is fallacious. The argument is that the word 'art' depends for its very meaning on there being a quality in common to its instances. But as we saw in an earlier chapter, the instances of a concept may be related by family resemblance rather than by having a quality in common. Thus there is no quality, or set of qualities, common to all games. Nevertheless the word 'game' has a perfectly clear meaning.

There is a fallacy also in Bell's argument to show that representational content has no artistic value. His argument is that art cannot be representational since photography is representational and photography is different from art. The fallacy here is of a common type. It involves a confusion between necessary and sufficient conditions. The most Bell's argument can show is that being representational is not a *sufficient* condition for art. Other activities also may be representational. It certainly does not follow that art cannot be representational at all. Here is a parallel argument where the fallacy will be evident: 'The Welsh cannot be British since the English are British and the English are different from the Welsh.' Being British is not sufficient to make one Welsh. It plainly does not follow that in being Welsh one cannot be British. Similarly, it does not follow that because being representational is not sufficient for artistic value, artistic value can never be representational.

It will be evident on reflection that if photography differs from art, that is not because one does and the other does not represent the world. The difference lies, rather, in the form that representation takes in the two cases. Thus the disadvantage in photography, from an artistic point of view, is that it reproduces mechanically the features of a scene, whether or not they are of artistic significance. No doubt an imaginative photographer can compensate to some extent for this disadvantage. But the greater freedom remains with the painter. For he is not at all tied to literal detail but can add one here or omit one there. Indeed, he can combine details from one scene with those from another, so long as he is imaginative in doing so. Painting, in short, allows greater freedom to the artistic imagination.

But throughout the history of European art, the imagination of the painter has been at work in representing the world. We may return to Rembrandt to illustrate the point. On Bell's view, his value as a portrait painter lies not in what he reveals about human character but in his compositional power. Here we have the same presupposition we found in Wilde. It is argued that the value of a work must lie *wholly* in its artistic treatment, because it does not lie *wholly* in its content. But as Tolstoy demonstrates, the dichotomy is a false one. The value of a portrait by Rembrandt lies in what through his compositional power he reveals about human character. The medium an artist adopts has its own forms. But they have their value in enabling that artist to reveal, not the forms themselves, but aspects of the world which in any other form we might never have noticed. Thus the doctrine of art for art's sake and the didactic theory rest on the same false presupposition. Remove the presupposition and they fall together.

There is, however, another theory, popular in the nineteenth century, which avoids that false presupposition. This is the romantic theory, to which we now turn.

**The Romantic Theory**

This theory has certain features in common with Tolstoy's own. Like his, it rejects both the doctrine of art for art's sake and the didactic theory, denying that art is separate from life and asserting the importance of artistic form. Moreover like his, it finds the connection between art and life in art's expressive function. We shall consider the theory as it was developed in the 1930s by R. G. Collingwood. Collingwood was a highly distinguished philosopher with a mastery of the English language. It will be interesting to consider how he develops his theory.

Before the nineteenth century art and craft were synonymous. People distinguished between the fine and the useful arts, the latter unlike the former being of immediate practical benefit. But that was a distinction between species of the same genus, or members of the same family. In the course of the nineteenth century, however, as we have remarked, there was a change in the role of the artist. The change was reflected in usage, art and craft being sharply distinguished. The point is directly relevant to Collingwood's main work in aesthetics, *The Principles of Art*.[9] In this work he begins with a theoretical formulation of the difference between art and craft, and much of the work depends on that theoretical basis. His view is that one cannot properly understand art, in theoretical terms, unless one has first distinguished it from a craft.

Thus he begins by listing the characteristics he takes to be distinctive of a craft. The most important are the following: (*a*) a craft always involves a distinction between means and end; (*b*) the end is preconceived or thought out before being arrived at; (*c*) in any craft there is a distinction between raw material and finished product, the skill of the craftsman lying precisely in his ability to fashion his product out of his raw material. Collingwood then takes poetry as an instance of art and argues that it is distinguishable from a craft in each of the above respects: (*a*) it allows no foothold for the distinction between means and end; for (*b*) the poet before writing his poem does not envisage what he will write; indeed if he could envisage it that clearly he would already have written it; (*c*) in the case of a poem there is no raw material out of which it is fashioned.

Having distinguished, in this way, between art and craft, Collingwood proceeds to argue that many activities having the appearance of art are really crafts. He distinguishes in particular between, on the one hand, amusement art and magic art and, on the other, art proper. The former have in common that they are representational and directed towards an end. Thus amusement art represents the world with the aim of diverting or entertaining; magic art represents the world with the aim of stimulating emotion for practical purposes. Collingwood's use of the term magic is somewhat eccentric. Stimulating emotion for practical purposes is for him not a necessary but a sufficient condition for applying the term. That enables him to identify practices so various as destroying the effigy of an enemy, laying a wreath on a grave, and participating in ballroom dancing as equally magical. Nevertheless his point is tolerably clear. He wishes to distinguish art proper from any activity which represents the world for some definite end.

The obvious objection to that view, as we have seen, is that it is difficult in the history of art to find a work that does not so represent the world. Collingwood's reply will be familiar to us. He does not deny that art may be representational, but only that its being representational is what makes it art. In other words, it may be both at once. It may be representational and artistic. The point is, however, that what makes it artistic is not what makes it representational. The resemblance here between Collingwood and Clive Bell will be evident. Indeed it would be difficult, so far, to distinguish Collingwood's theory from the doctrine of art for art's sake.

Nevertheless there is an important difference. Collingwood preserves a connection with life. It lies in the relation between art and the artist. Roughly speaking, art is an expression of the artist's feelings. Thus Rembrandt's greatness as a painter lies not in his ability to represent the character of his sitter but in his ability to express his feelings on contemplating that character. His painting, artistically considered, is an exercise in the expression and therefore clarification of emotion.

Here Collingwood's theory may remind us of Tolstoy's. Let us be clear, however, that his theory is not Tolstoy's own. Thus, for Collingwood, a work of art does not exist in the mode of communication. In other words, the artist does not represent life with the aim of showing others what he feels about it. His work consists in his expressing what he feels in order to make it clear to himself. Indeed, in the first part of his book, Collingwood takes this view to the extreme pitch of subjectivism. For example, he says that the expression of emotion, simply as expression, is not addressed to any particular audience. Where an audience is present, when an artist expresses himself, they are in the position of persons who overhear him doing this.[10]

But before we are in a position to evaluate Collingwood's theory, we must consider in more detail what he means by the expression of emotion. He distinguishes expressing an emotion from betraying it. To betray an emotion is simply to exhibit it, as when a child lashes out in anger. To express an emotion, by contrast, is in some measure to master or understand it. On Collingwood's view, an emotion, in its beginnings, is confused or unclear. It is in the process of expressing one's emotion that one becomes clear about it. Indeed, he seems to go further and to suggest that the emotion, as a definite state, does not exist until it has been expressed or clarified, so that an emotion is inextricably involved with its expression.

We now find a move which has about it the appearance of inconsistency. Earlier, in distinguishing between art and craft, Collingwood had taken as essential to art that it does *not* involve the transformation of a material. This gave his account, as we have seen, an appearance of extreme subjectivity. Moreover, the subjectivity was explicitly affirmed. For example, Collingwood affirms, earlier in his book, that the painter's canvas is incidental to his art. His art, strictly speaking, exists not on his canvas but in his mind. It now appears, however, that the artistic medium, so far from being incidental to art, is in fact essential to it. Since an emotion, in its existence as a definite state, is inextricably involved with its expression, it requires for its existence some medium in which it can be expressed. The painter's medium is paint on canvas. Consequently, it is *in* his painting on canvas that he expresses his emotion and thereby creates his art.

This view has a startling implication. Art must be essentially particular. Since the painter's emotion, as a definite state, is inextricably involved with his work on *this* canvas then independently of *this* canvas, it cannot exist. It follows that each work of art is unique, not in the sense that it expresses a common emotion in its own distinctive way, but in the sense that the emotion it expresses is entirely particular to itself. The artist, says Collingwood, 'does not want a thing of a certain kind, he wants a certain thing'.[11] For example, a painter in expressing sadness is expressing not sadness of a certain type but the one which is inextricably involved with the canvas he is painting, and were we to inquire which sadness this might be, he could only say 'This one', pointing to his canvas.

It is not difficult to understand and to sympathize with what Collingwood seeks to achieve in his account of expression in art. He seeks to liberate art from the sterile assumptions of nineteenth-century aestheticism. To do this, he must achieve two other aims. He must do justice to the relation between art and life, but only by doing justice also to artistic form. He seems correct in both these aims. He seems correct also in assuming that he will best achieve them by concentrating on art in its expressive function. But there are surely difficulties in his account of the expressive function. As we have seen, for example, he is an extreme nominalist. Art, in short, is essentially particular. It is not, as in Tolstoy, the particular expression of some feeling itself universal. It is the particular expression of a particular feeling, namely, the one it expresses itself. The effect of this view is to obscure rather than to elucidate the relation between art and life. For how can a work have any relation to life, if what is expresses exists nowhere outside itself? The view, in its effect, seems indistinguishable from the doctrine of art for art's sake. As Aristotle said, art has its value in giving particular expression to the universal. *What* is expressed, therefore, in all great art is universal, therein lies its greatness. It is only the *way* it expresses the universal that is particular. It follows that particularity in art has value only where it has a significance which surpasses itself. Shakespeare's *Macbeth*, for example, teaches us about life because it expresses a corruption only too common in life. It would teach us nothing were it to express a corruption peculiar to itself.

Before the nineteenth century, the artist conformed, more or less, to the classical view of art. On this view, art is an impersonal discipline, being the creation of no individual, through which one may learn to express oneself but only by repeated attempts, usually approximate or incomplete, to meet the demands, not of one's emotions, but of the discipline itself. On this view, art and craft, on points vital to both, are indistinguishable. For both are disciplines which can be mastered only by long and arduous work. Haydn at the end of his life said that he knew at last how to write for the woodwind. There was a motto common to both: life is short; art is long. The subjective for both was an enemy, for art or craft, being a discipline, is objective. Spontaneity or freedom of expression, for example, was valued only as the reward for a discipline mastered, as in the case of the great artist or master craftsman for whom the exercise of his skill had become as easy as breathing. Otherwise it was not simply valueless but worse, an element disruptive of that discipline without which there would be no art or craft. Work, on this conception, must be judged by those for whom it is intended. It requires an audience qualified to judge its products, for otherwise it is liable to the bias, and therefore corruption, of those who produce them. The writer, as Johnson expressed it, must submit himself to the judgement of the common reader. In both art and craft, the concrete or particular was inferior to the general or universal; for a detail is superfluous unless it performs some function and the function must derive its significance from something more general than any detail. In the story of Joseph, we may remember, not a detail is superfluous, for each serves to further the story, which expresses a theme more universal than any story taken in itself.

These values were reversed, in the course of the nineteenth century, by the Romantic movement. Spontaneity, as such, came to be valued above craft or technique, which was relegated to a lower non-artistic category. The artist came to be treated as superior to his audience. The concrete or particular was valued above the general or universal. Now it is these values which seem to be reflected throughout the first two-thirds of Collingwood's book. Early in the book he gives the example of an artist who without conscious purpose is fingering a ball of clay. Suddenly the clay under his fingers begins to turn into a figure. We are not told whether this artist, in apparent spontaneity, is exercising a skill he has in fact acquired through arduous labour. He exists in a void. His art is sheer spontaneity. Moreover, we are told that this example provides a key to the very nature of art. In elucidating art, Collingwood excludes the audience and concentrates on the artist. It is only in the last part of the book, and with apparent inconsistency, that the audience figures as an important element in the artistic process. Collingwood's preference for the concrete or particular is taken, as we have seen, to an extreme of nominalism.

But it is in his treatment of craft or technique that Collingwood seems most evidently to betray the influence of Romanticism. These are associated throughout with a mechanical repetitiveness. He acknowledges that technique is not incompatible with art. But it belongs to those aspects of a work which are non-artistic. To reveal the artistic aspects, one must exclude the technical ones. The relation between means and end is treated throughout in its simplest or most impoverished form. For Collingwood, a means depends wholly on its end for whatever value it may possess. A means, in short, has no value in itself. Craftsmanship is such a means, deriving its value wholly from the end it achieves. Craftsmanship, in short, has no value in itself. It follows, since the category of means and end exists only in this impoverished form, that it cannot be applied to art. One consequence of this is that the artist, *qua* artist, cannot have the aim of representing the world. He cannot have any aim or end, *qua* artist, for then his work would have no value in itself.

Tolstoy, it is true, is critical of craft or technique where it has become cheap or mechanical. But in that form it is a degradation of craft no less than of art. Moreover the basis of Tolstoy's account is classical, as is evident in his defence of universality and of the importance of an audience. Collingwood's account, by contrast, moves within the categories of Romanticism. We must emphasize that this is not of deliberate intent. Indeed, he spends the last part of his book in attempting to avoid the implications of what he has written in the first two-thirds. Unfortunately, the categories of Romanticism are so embedded in his account that he can avoid their implications only at the cost of inconsistency. Our conclusion at this stage, therefore, is that Collingwood has failed to liberate art from the sterility of nineteenth-century assumptions, because he has accepted too many of these assumptions himself.

We must now test that conclusion by returning to the details of his account. We must look, in particular, at its basis, namely, the contrast between art and craft. We may note that the contrast depends heavily on a single example, that of poetry. Collingwood states, for example, that poetry, unlike the crafts, does not depend on the transformation of a raw material. This is true, but one may wonder what it reveals. On reflection, it seems to reveal less about art than about the special nature of poetry or literature. The poet works in words. The essence of a word is in its use, not in its physical substance. The reason one cannot specify a physical substance for poetry is that in its essence it is not physical. In that respect, however, it differs not simply from the crafts but from every other art. For example, if a sculptor works in stone, there can be little difficulty in specifying the raw material with which he works. There seems as little in specifying the end to which he fashions his material. He produces a statue. The statue is the end product; the stone is the raw material out of which he fashions it. Moreover, the sculptor's end in fashioning his material seems to have a place in ends other than his own, for, traditionally at least, he has supplied his product for decoration, for amusement, for use in various ceremonies, religious or secular, and so on.

Collingwood, perhaps, would say that the sculptor does not fashion his material according to a preconceived plan. But that, even if true, would not distinguish the sculptor from many who practise a skill or craft. Boxing, for example, is normally treated as a skill or craft. But the boxer's skill does not consist in carrying out a sequence of movements determined beforehand. That only happens when a fight is fixed. Usually a boxer works out what to do as he goes along, though this spontaneity, we may note, is the product of a discipline painfully acquired. But further: many deemed artists work more evidently to a preconceived plan than do many craftsmen. Thus ballet-dancers, actors, singers, concert pianists and conductors all work with predetermined scripts or scores. Laurence Olivier, for example, was deemed an artist. But his art lay precisely in his ability to translate a text into spoken word and gesture. It may be said that his artistry lay in his interpretative power, which cannot be reduced to rules or wholly specified beforehand. But in that respect he would differ only in degree from any craftsman whose work rises above the mindlessly mechanical. As we have said, for example, two cooks following exactly the same recipe may still produce different dishes, one much finer than the other. In short, the best cooking depends on details too fine to be formulated. In fact, none of the traditional crafts depended on formulatable rules. They were acquired through experience and allowed countless opportunities for the exercise of improvisation and ingenuity.[12]

None of the above remarks implies, let it be noted, that there are no important differences among the arts and crafts. Such differences are readily available on the traditional conception. For example, the so-called fine arts, such as poetry and music, differ from many crafts in not supplying an immediate need, and differ also from the amusement arts in offering something more than amusement. But these are the differences which hold, as we have said, among different species of a genus or members of a family. In passing from one to another we do not cross a gulf, finding ourselves on the other side with radically different concepts. The resemblances are just as important as the differences. On Collingwood's conception, by contrast, it is only the differences that are important; the resemblances hardly exist.

In fairness to Collingwood, however, we must remark that he has been vigorously defended against the above criticisms. For example, Aaron Ridley, in a lively and interesting work, has argued that it is idle to make exceptions to Collingwood's contrast between craft and art.[13] For, on Ridley's view, he never attempted to show that art *cannot* have the properties of a craft but only that it *need* not have them. This interpretation, were it correct, would happily rescue Collingwood from the confusions in which he seems to be involved. But it is very difficult to accept it as correct. Collingwood certainly does allow that a work may have aspects both of craft and art. In short, a work, *otherwise* artistic, may have the properties of a craft. But he does not allow that art, *qua* art, can have those properties. Thus, as we have seen, he allows that a representational work may be artistic but denies that it can be artistic *in* being representational.

It is relevant, in this connection, to consider the many apparent inconsistencies in Collingwood's book. As we have seen, for example, he gives the impression in the first half of his book that the artistic medium is incidental to art itself, which exists entirely in the artist's mind; later it transpires that the artistic medium is essential to the artistic process. There are many such examples. On page 111, for example, Collingwood writes as follows about the artist: 'If what he wishes to do is to express his emotions intelligibly, he has to express them in such a way as to be intelligible to himself; his audience is then in the position of persons who overhear him doing this.' There is a footnote to the effect that this view will later be modified. On page 322 we find: 'A careful study of such things will convince anyone who is open to conviction that the position of the audience is very far from being that of a licensed eavesdropper, overhearing something that would be complete without him.' On any reading, the second statement does not modify but flatly contradicts the first. Collingwood here denies what he himself has affirmed.

These inconsistencies can be explained, in my view, only as a consequence of his attempting at the start of his book to make a radical contrast between art and craft. This contrast can be sustained only by denying to art properties which are in fact essential to it. In consequence, Collingwood, in giving a positive account of art, is forced to bring back the properties earlier denied. Earlier, by contrast with the craftsman, the artist does not have the aim of communicating with an audience. Later, the audience being in fact essential to art, it is brought back in the role of collaborator. Strictly speaking, that is absurd. In what sense, for example, in reading *Hamlet* do I collaborate with Shakespeare? But Collingwood is forced into this position by having attempted to sustain a radical contrast between art and craft.

There is, it is true, an alternative view among the commentators. Some have argued that Collingwood's apparent inconsistencies are due simply to looseness of expression.[14] But there is in fact no looseness of expression. It is entirely precise. Here, for example, is Collingwood contrasting the artist proper with the craftsman:

> His business is not to produce an emotional effect in his audience but, for example, to make a tune. This tune is already complete and perfect when it exists merely as a tune in his head, that is an imaginary tune. Next, he may arrange for the tune to be played before an audience. Now there comes into existence a real tune, a collection of noises. But which of these two things is the work of art? Which of them is the music? The answer is implied in what we have already said: the music, the work of art, is not the collection of noises, it is the tune in the composer's head. The noises made by the performers and heard by the audience, are not the music at all ...[15]

The view here expressed is that music, as a proper art, can be distinguished from a craft in that it has no essential connection with the physical medium of sound. It is hard to see how anyone could state the view more precisely.

John Dewey argued that the conception of means and end common among philosophers was so false to the actual relation, so impoverished in itself, that it could be explained only on sociological ground.[16] His explanation was that it reflected the degraded state into which craftsmanship had fallen during the course of the nineteenth century. He had in mind the way the older crafts were replaced by machines. Machine work was so mindlessly repetitive that no sane human being could value it in itself. It could be valued only for what it produced, in short, for its end. Here, Dewey thought, was the source of the idea that a means without its end would be devoid of value. He would surely have thought that his remarks apply to Collingwood's account in *The Principles of Art*. As we have seen, Collingwood takes for granted that a means derives its value wholly from its end. In fact, an end is most effectively achieved where its means also has a value. For example, a person usually becomes better at his work the more he comes to like it. That he likes it in itself enables him the better to achieve its end. Indeed there are some ends which cannot be achieved in any other way. In other words, unless one attributes independent value to the means, one cannot achieve such an end. For example, I may choose to go to a concert because I know the music will give me an enjoyable evening. But it cannot give me an enjoyable evening unless I value the music itself and not simply the enjoyment it gives me. It makes sense to tolerate tedious music for certain ends but hardly for the end of enjoying oneself. The point is important in connection with art, because art achieves its purposes precisely by arousing interest in itself.

In holding so impoverished a conception of means and end, Collingwood is led to a view of art which is the exact opposite of Tolstoy's. Thus, on Collingwood's view, art proper is not intended to have an effect on its audience; it is not intended, for example, to evoke or to stimulate feelings. Activities having such an end belong to magic or amusement, not to art proper. To support this view, he makes a contrast between the artist and the comedian or funny man. The aim of the latter is to make an audience laugh. If he fails in this aim, he is a bad comedian. By contrast, a work of art may fail to have an effect on its audience and still be good as art. It follows, on Collingwood's view, that what makes it good as art is distinct from its having an effect on its audience. This argument, however, is unsound. A comedian who fails to make an audience laugh is not thereby a bad one. The fault may lie not with him but with his audience. They may lack the wit to grasp his jokes. Now, similarly, if you claim that a work which has failed in its effect on an audience is nevertheless good, you can only be taken to imply that the audience failed to grasp the effect intended and that had it grasped that effect, the work would not have failed. It is difficult to know what else you could mean in calling the work good. In other words, Collingwood's argument does not show that a work's having an effect on an audience is irrelevant to what makes it good as art. All it shows is that a work may be good without having an effect on every type of audience or under all conditions.

We may illustrate the same point by reference to the common distinction between art and propaganda. The difference between the two is *not* that the propagandist, unlike the artist, seeks to affect an audience. The difference lies in the effects they seek to achieve and the means they adopt to achieve them. The propagandist, for example, seeks for an immediate effect and will cheapen or falsify his material in order to achieve it. The true artist, by contrast, is more scrupulous in handling his material. But just for that reason he can achieve effects which are impossible to the propagandist. Those effects which tolerate cheapness in the means are cheap effects; those which tolerate falsification in the means have about them a certain falsity. For that reason, the propagandist is incapable of complexity and profundity. For certain purposes art is a more effective device than propaganda.

Collingwood's conception of means and end has its influence, also, on his account of artistic expression. Here, again, his account differs strikingly from

Tolstoy's. As we have seen, Tolstoy distinguishes between two types of what he calls infection, the artistic and the instinctive. Artistic infection presupposes the instinctive but transforms it through the conscious use of symbols. The primitive relation of means and end, as it exists in instinctive infection, is thereby transformed in the artistic process. An audience is infected in artistic terms, for example, only where it gives conscious attention to the work of art itself. But the relation between means and end, though transformed, is not abolished. The work of art is a means by which, for example, people's attention may be drawn to aspects of the world they might not otherwise have noticed. Nor does it follow that the work is valueless in itself, deriving its value wholly from those aspects to which it draws attention. For it would not have drawn attention to those aspects had it not aroused conscious interest in itself.

Collingwood's account, in the beginning, is not dissimilar to Tolstoy's. For example, his distinction between betraying and expressing an emotion is comparable with Tolstoy's distinction between instinctive and artistic infection. But for Collingwood the artistic process altogether transcends the relation between means and end. In consequence, he can attribute to art only those purposes which are internal to the artistic process. This means that a work can express nothing more general than itself. A work expresses, as Collingwood put it, not a certain kind of thing but a certain thing. The certain thing can be indicated only by pointing to the work itself.

To remove the confusion in this account, let us return to Aristotle's view that art gives particular expression to the universal. A simple example will illustrate what he meant. Suppose an artist sketches a smiling face. The sketch is, as it were, a symbol of human happiness. But suppose you are now asked whose happiness the drawing represents. If you are thinking entirely along the line of the particular, you will be thrown by that question. For the drawing seems not to represent anyone's happiness in particular. You may be tempted to attribute it to the artist. But, as Tolstoy says, the work may be imaginary. In the end, there seems no particular left but the drawing. So you are tempted to say that the drawing expresses itself.

If you think entirely in particular terms you are bound to get into that confusion. But you need not have done so. It will be evident on reflection that the representative relation is general not particular. The drawing, it is true, is a particular object but in its representative function it is inherently general. In this, it is anologous to a diagram in geometry. Suppose I draw a circle to illustrate a theorem. Someone now asks which circle that represents. The question is absurd since the drawing represents *any* such circle. The analogy with art is a real one.[17] For example, suppose an artist adds a touch of malice to the smile in his drawing. Suddenly you remember having seen that expression many times and now you see it more clearly. But does it follow that the artist was representing the specific people you remember? It is altogether unlikely that he had seen any of them. But then he had no need to do so. For he had caught *the type*.

Having caught the type, he could leave you to find the instances for yourself. It is in this way that we learn from art. We can learn from the smile in the drawing, because it catches a type of malice which exists outside.

A real example may reinforce the point. Wilfred Owen wished to express the horror and pity of war. He sought to achieve this aim through poetry, through concrete image rather than general statement. But the images, though less abstract, were just as general in their significance as any statement. For it was war itself, not this or that detail, that he sought to express in its pity and horror. The details were significant only so far as they expressed a general understanding. This was an understanding which, through their experience of war, had come to others as well as to himself. It was therefore essential to him that his poetry should express what existed independently of his own artistic expression. For he sought to express only what others understood who could not express it for themselves. Moreover, we should deceive ourselves if we thought that our understanding of war, acquired through Owen's poetry, is therefore superior to the understanding of others who acquired theirs through experience.

In fact Owen's poetry often convinces in spite of its artistic expression. He fell in the war before his talent had fully developed. What convinces is his sincerity. It is the quality Tolstoy valued above all others. Nor in order to judge Owen's sincerity do we need to check the details of his life. It is expressed in his poetry which throughout is that of a man who knows and feels the horror of what he relates.

We have been selective in discussing Collingwood's account of art.[18] There are passages we have not discussed which are interesting and important. In any case, as we have said, he attempts at the end of his book to avoid some of the implications of his main account. But it is the main account, and its implications, that has concerned us. It is a sophisticated version of the romantic theory, which, together with the doctrine of art for art's sake, was the main rival in the nineteenth century to Tolstoy's own. Tolstoy's own account, we have argued, is superior to both.

## Notes

1 Yvor Winters, *In Defence of Reason*, Denver, Swallow Press, 1947, pp. 3–14. Winters refers specifically to theories of literature. But for our purpose we may take him to be referring to theories of art in general.
2 Ibid., p. 4.
3 Ibid., p. 6.
4 Collected by Richard Ellmann in *The Artist as Critic*, London, W. H. Allen, 1970.
5 Ibid., pp. 235–6. I have selected the remarks that are most relevant to our purpose.
6 Ibid., p. 248.
7 Clive Bell, *Art*, London, Chatto and Windus, 1949, p. 7.

8   Ibid., p. 7.
9   R. G. Collingwood, *The Principles of Art*, Oxford, OUP, 1958.
10  Ibid., p. 111.
11  Ibid., p. 114.
12  It will be relevant, in this connection, to quote some of John Haldane's comments on architecture: 'In philosophical aesthetics it has been common for writers to draw a distinction between art and craft. The limitations of this distinction soon become apparent, however, when one considers architecture, for the attempt to locate an understanding of this within the art/craft dichotomy results in such absurdities as that buildings should be thought of as inhabitable sculptures, or else viewed as decorated habitation machines. In fact, architecture provides a particularly powerful refutation of the idea that aesthetic value is one thing and practical function another.' 'Form, Meaning and Value: A History of the Philosophy of Architecture', *The Journal of Architecture*, vol. 4, Spring 1999, p. 9.
13  A. Ridley, *R. G. Collingwood*, London, Phoenix, 1998, pp. 12–13.
14  See, for example, R. Sclafani, 'Wollheim on Collingwood', *Philosophy*, vol. 51, 1976, pp. 353–9.
15  Collingwood, *The Principles of Art*, p. 139.
16  I have discussed Dewey's view in more detail in *The Two Pragmatisms*, London, Routledge, 1997, pp. 131–3.
17  A real analogy does not preclude real differences at other points. For example, the interest in a diagram usually does not reside at all in itself but in what one can do with it. In that respect there is a significant difference from art.
18  For a more positive assessment of Collingwood's account see the works, already cited, by Ridley and Sclafani. See also two papers by Peter Lewis: 'Art, the Community's Medicine', *The British Journal of Aesthetics*, vol. 35, no. 3, 1995, pp. 205–15, and 'Collingwood on Art and Fantasy', *Philosophy*, vol. 64, 1989, pp. 547–56.

CHAPTER ELEVEN

# Shakespeare

Before concluding our account of Tolstoy's views on art, we must consider his famous criticism of Shakespeare. This is contained, principally, in his essay 'Shakespeare and the Drama'.[1] The essay is interesting, for our purpose, because it throws additional light on *What is Art?*. For example, it contains Tolstoy's most explicit repudiation of the didactic theory. In my view, it is also of great interest in itself. My own view, it is true, is not widely shared among the commentators. In 1947, George Orwell claimed in a well-known essay that Tolstoy's criticism of Shakespeare is based not on reasoned argument but on personal antipathy and religious prejudice.[2] He has been very influential. Some hold, indeed, that Tolstoy's essay on Shakespeare is the most perverse of all his works. We shall endeavour to show that this attitude is mistaken. The work is of considerable power and within its own terms of reference entirely successful. It does not follow that we should accept its conclusion. That would follow only if we accepted the terms of reference. These are determined by the standards of Tolstoy's own art, the realistic novel. But Tolstoy was very far from arbitrary in his terms of reference. They were shared at the time by many who were enthusiastic in their praise of Shakespeare. They are shared by many who read Shakespeare in our own day. We have already noted that Tolstoy often says only what we have thought ourselves and could also have said, except that we lacked his courage. The quality is pervasive in his writings. But it is pre-eminent in his essay on Shakespeare. In that respect, it is one of the most liberating of his works. It seems to me indispensable to any serious student of Shakespeare. Anyone who reads it with attention will find that he needs to make clearer to himself wherein lies Shakespeare's greatness. For he will know with certainty wherein it does *not* lie.[3]

We must begin with Orwell's essay 'Lear, Tolstoy and the Fool'. As we have said, it has served to prejudice innumerable readers against Tolstoy's essay. It is necessary to remove that prejudice. Orwell opens by saying that since Tolstoy's essay is not readily available he will summarize its contents. In fact he summarizes in any detail only the first twenty-eight pages, which constitute roughly a quarter of the whole. In these pages Tolstoy says that he wishes to concentrate on *King Lear*, as representing what is commonly agreed to be Shakespeare at his greatest, and proceeds to give an account of its plot. Orwell quotes from Tolstoy's account and complains, with some justice, that it is not impartial. He then deals briefly with Tolstoy's general criticism of Shakespeare and with his attempt to explain Shakespeare's popularity. Having summarized Tolstoy's essay, at least to his own satisfaction, Orwell proceeds as follows:

> This, then, is the substance of Tolstoy's pamphlet. One's first feeling is that in describing Shakespeare as a bad writer he is saying something demonstrably untrue. But this is not the case. In reality there is no kind of evidence or argument by which one can show that Shakespeare or any other writer is 'good'. Nor is there any way of definitely proving that – for instance – Warwick Deeping is 'bad'. Ultimately there is no test of literary merit except survival, which is itself an index to majority opinion. Artistic theories such as Tolstoy's are quite worthless, because they not only start out with arbitrary assumptions, but depend on vague terms ('sincere', 'important', and so forth) which can be interpreted in any way one chooses. Properly speaking one cannot *answer* Tolstoy's attack. The interesting question is: why did he make it?[4]

On Orwell's view, it is meaningless to ask whether Shakespeare has survived *because* he is good, as distinct from some other reason. Since he has survived, he must be 'good', in the only intelligible sense. Orwell's view is no doubt sincerely held, but it has the consequence that he need give no serious consideration to Tolstoy's *arguments*. Contrary to the impression he conveys, these are very numerous. For example, within the first twenty-eight pages, in discussing *King Lear*, Tolstoy makes detailed reference not simply to apparent implausibilities in its characterization but to many apparent inconsistencies in its plot. Orwell does mention in passing that many of these arguments are 'weak or dishonest'. But he makes no serious attempt to demonstrate either their dishonesty or their weakness.[5] His essay, so far, has occupied four pages. Any attempt at literary criticism ends at this point. The remaining fourteen pages of the essay are given over to psychological analysis. The question is not whether Tolstoy's criticism is true but why he made it.

In pursuit of an answer, Orwell raises the question of why, when he had some thirty of Shakespeare's works to choose from, Tolstoy should have chosen *King Lear* in particular. Tolstoy supplies an answer to that question at the beginning of his essay: Shakespeare wrote some thirty works, but not all of them are masterpieces and Tolstoy wishes to tackle him at his best. *King Lear* by common agreement is among the greatest of his works and many consider it the greatest of them all. Orwell brushes aside this response. It seems to him likely that Tolstoy, in conducting a hostile analysis, should pick on a work he especially dislikes. The question is why he especially dislikes it. 'Is it not possible,' Orwell asks, 'that he bore an especial enmity towards this play because he was aware, consciously or unconsciously, of the resemblance between Lear's story and his own?'[6]

Now those of us who do not exactly like this line of inquiry may nevertheless feel confident at this stage that we know where it leads. Orwell is going to indicate those striking resemblances between Lear and Tolstoy himself which have served, though perhaps unconsciously, to arouse Tolstoy's resentment. In this, however, we are deceived. Orwell is remarkably evasive about where precisely these resemblances lie. His approach is to scatter suggestions, rather in the manner of a marksman who scatters bullets at a target in the hope that one will hit it. He asks us, for example, to close our eyes and attend to the image that *King Lear* suggests to us:

> Here at any rate is what I see; a majestic old man in a long black robe, with flowing white hair and beard, a figure out of Blake's drawings (but also, curiously enough, rather like Tolstoy) wandering through a storm and cursing the heavens, in company with a Fool and a lunatic.[7]

Orwell here, I assume, is relying on photographs of Tolstoy in old age which readers of his generation would recall having seen in the newspapers. But the suggestion is no sooner made than it is dropped. He makes very little of the real resemblance between Tolstoy and Lear. For example, both having renounced their estates, died in flight. He seems uneasily aware that the resemblances, on closer inspection, will prove unsuitable for his purpose. Thus the reasons for renunciation in the two cases are entirely different. Moreover, Tolstoy's flight occurred after he wrote his essay on Shakespeare, so it can hardly constitute substantial evidence for his motive in writing it.

Eventually we arrive on firmer ground, but it is not quite the one we anticipated. It transpires that the cause of Tolstoy's resentment is not so much the resemblance between Lear and himself as the conflict between the theme of Shakespeare's play and his own religious beliefs. Orwell presents this as a conflict between humanism and religion. The theme of *King Lear* is humanist. It says in effect:

> 'Give away your lands if you want to, but don't expect to gain happiness by doing so. Probably you won't gain happiness. If you live for others, you must live *for others*, and not as a roundabout way of getting an advantage for yourself.'[8]

On Orwell's view Tolstoy's attitude is the opposite. For him, virtue involves renunciation but with the aim of ultimate happiness. In this he is typically religious. For the religious attitude finds its motive not in struggling with the evils of this life but in attaining the Kingdom of Heaven. In the end, it is self-interested and hedonistic. The humanist, by contrast, is committed to this life, whether or not it brings happiness. Only the humanist can appreciate tragedy.

Orwell supports the above views by an analysis of Tolstoy's character. He acknowledges that Tolstoy was not a vulgar hypocrite but detects a more sinister vice. He says of such people as Tolstoy: 'There is always the possibility – the probability, indeed – that they have done no more than exchange one form of egoism for another.'[9] Within a few sentences probability has become certainty. Orwell explains in some detail that we should not be taken in by people who appear virtuous. Such people might be worse than we are, not because they are wicked in the vulgar sense, but because they have taken pride in their own virtue. Moreover spiritual pride carries other vices in its train. Thinking themselves wholly in the right, the spiritually proud do not hesitate in bullying people into thinking as they do. Such is the case with Tolstoy.

It is worth noting that Orwell delivers these remarks about spiritual pride as though they constituted an insight unavailable to the religious themselves. Spiritual pride is the sin perhaps most often condemned by the Gospels. Orwell is merely repeating what is expressed with incomparably greater power in the parable of the Pharisee and the sinner. Spiritual pride is analysed with masterly power by Tolstoy himself in *Father Sergius*, one of the greatest of his late works. It is obvious that Tolstoy could have been affected with the pride he analysed in others. Elementary charity would suggest, however, that this might have been obvious also to Tolstoy.

Now Tolstoy in his essay implies that his view of Shakespeare has not been determined by his religious conversion. He says on his first page, for example, that he has held his view over many years. Later he reports conversations, that could only have occurred many years earlier, with Turgenev and Fet, in which he attempted unsuccessfully to persuade them of his view. This claim, were it true, would undermine Orwell's interpretation. It is only on the last page of his essay that Orwell considers it. He responds as follows:

> We may be sure that in his unregenerate days Tolstoy's conclusion would have been, 'You like Shakespeare – I don't. Let's leave it at that'. Later, when his perception that it takes all sorts to make a world had deserted him, he came to think of Shakespeare's writings as something dangerous to himself. The more pleasure people took in Shakespeare, the less they would listen to Tolstoy. Therefore nobody must be *allowed* to enjoy Shakespeare, just as nobody must be allowed to drink alcohol or smoke tobacco. True, Tolstoy would not prevent them by force. He is not demanding that the police shall impound every copy of Shakespeare's works. But he will do dirt on Shakespeare if he can. He will try to get inside the mind of every lover of Shakespeare and kill his enjoyment by every trick he can think of, including – as I have shown in my summary of his pamphlet – arguments which are self-contradictory or even doubtfully honest.[10]

We may agree, I trust, that the tendency to impute bad motives to one's opponent is a regrettable one. The motives that Orwell imputes to Tolstoy are undoubtedly bad, as a glance at the last paragraph will confirm. He would still be justified had he conclusive or even solid evidence for the motives he imputes. It is demonstrable that he has no such evidence. It is a mere fantasy to claim, as does Orwell, that Tolstoy was motivated by religious prejudice to do dirt on Shakespeare.

Tolstoy was a voluminous diarist. He left a record of his life stretching from early manhood to old age. His diaries contain a number of references to Shakespeare. The earliest direct references are on 24 and 31 January 1856, when Tolstoy was in his late twenties. On those days, he was present among a group of intellectuals who had gathered to hear a translation of *King Lear*. During these meetings most members of the group, but especially Turgenev, attempted to dispel Tolstoy's dislike of Shakespeare. They were unsuccessful. In short, the diaries confirm what Tolstoy says in his essay. It is perhaps significant that the subject of that meeting, which Tolstoy remembered all his life, was *King Lear*. There are references to Shakespeare in every subsequent decade of Tolstoy's life and they are almost invariably unfavourable. George Gibian, who has carefully sifted the record, summarizes his conclusion in the following terms, making specific reference to 'Shakespeare and the Drama':

> That essay is the most important and only formal statement of Tolstoy's hostility to Shakespeare. Tolstoy wrote it in 1903, at a time when he had formed definite aesthetic and religious views and when his numerous eccentric opinions on various subjects had become widely known. From the date of writing, we might easily be misled into thinking that Tolstoy's anti-Shakespearean treatise was inspired by one of the freakish prejudices of his old age, and that in his youth, before his conversion and transformation into a religious leader and prophet, the author of *War and Peace* and *Anna Karenina* may have held different, far more favourable views about Shakespeare. This assumption would not be correct, however. It would be inaccurate even in the division of Tolstoy's life and work into two widely separated phases, the early artistic, and the later religious and moral. The change in Tolstoy was far from clear-cut; there was much of the prophet and moralist in Tolstoy's youth, the so-called artistic period, just as there remained much of the artist in him during his later prophetic period.
>
> In so far as the supposition concerns Tolstoy's opinions on Shakespeare, it is definitely erroneous. Those who have spoken of Tolstoy's hatred for Shakespeare as if it had been restricted to his later years have not been aware of the record of Tolstoy's life-long expression of opinions about Shakespeare. An examination of that record ... shows that even in his youth and middle age, Tolstoy was bitterly opposed to Shakespeare.'[11]

It is time to turn our attentions to the details of Tolstoy's essay. As we have seen, in his first eight pages, Tolstoy summarizes the plot of *King Lear*. Orwell is correct in saying that the summary is not impartial, not at least in the sense that criticism is withheld until the plot is independently summarized. As usual, allowing his opponent no quarter, Tolstoy plunges straight into criticism. But let us attend to it. It falls into two categories. In the first are improbabilities of characterization. We may take as an example Tolstoy's comments on a scene crucial to the whole plot. Lear proposes to divide his kingdom among his daughters. To determine how much of his kingdom should be distributed to each, he asks them to declare in public how much they love him. Two of his daughters are profuse in their expression of love. Cordelia, his favourite, refuses to follow them. At this, Lear falls into a rage and curses his favourite daughter. Kent, a courtier who attempts to defend her, is immediately banished under threat of death. Cordelia is disinherited and her portion distributed among the other daughters. Tolstoy says that the scene is entirely improbable. No man would judge the character of his daughters, whom he already knows well, on the basis of what they would declare in public on a single occasion. It is impossible, therefore, to believe in a character who on that basis disinherits his favourite daughter. I suspect that many of us have had the same thought.

The second category involves inconsistencies or improbabilities in the plot. For example, as we noted, Kent the courtier is banished. In consequence, he assumes a disguise. Thereafter he becomes entirely unrecognizable not simply to comparative strangers but even to intimate acquaintances whom he engages in close conversation. Tolstoy's criticisms in this category depend on their cumulative effect. The following quotations merely indicate his approach:

> Edgar comes out of the hovel, and though they all know him, nobody recognizes him any more than they recognize Kent. (p. 322)
> Then, curiously enough, to the very spot on the open heath where he is, comes his father, blind Gloucester, led by an old man ... (p. 324)
> Gloucester is walking on level ground, but Edgar assures him that they are with difficulty ascending a steep hill. Gloucester believes this. (pp. 327–8)
> Lear says 'Pass!' and the blind Gloucester, who did not recognize his son's or Kent's voice, recognizes the King's. (p. 329)
> Edgar, with his stave, kills Oswald, who when dying gives Edgar (the man who has killed him) Goneril's letter to Edmund, the delivery of which will earn a reward. (p. 330)

Tolstoy prepared for his essay on Shakespeare with his usual indefatigable energy and thoroughness. Not only did he read all Shakespeare's works, in several languages, but he made a careful study of the sources on which Shakespeare drew for his major plays. In one of his most effective sections, he shows that Shakespeare often makes a bad job of adapting his sources, because he omits vital information. A good example is the scene in which Lear commands his daughters to declare their love for him. In the original play, this is not intended as a serious test but as a formal device for the transference of power. Lear takes for granted that Cordelia will go through with the ceremony and intends, when she has done so, to use it in order to get her betrothed to someone he favours. When she refuses to do this, he is not simply humiliated in public but trapped by his other daughters into taking seriously what he had intended as a mere device. Here Lear's motivation is clear and plausible throughout.

As Tolstoy shows, the same process has occurred in other plays. For example, Hamlet's madness has proved a puzzle for generations of readers and commentators. In the original, there is no puzzle, because it is assigned a clear motive. Hamlet, in dangerous circumstances, feigns madness in order to escape harm. Again, in *Othello*, Iago is assigned three different motives for his malignant behaviour. To assign a character three different motives is equivalent to assigning him none. For the audience is left with no clear sense of what moves him. In the original, Iago is assigned one clear motive: he is passionately in love with Desdemona.

It will be useful now to consider how Tolstoy formulates his main charges against Shakespeare. His first is that Shakespeare's plays do not develop according to a natural or inherent logic. He gives as an example from *King Lear* the relations between Gloucester and his sons which at numerous points are parallel to those between Lear and his daughters. The trouble is that Gloucester and his sons seem to be introduced simply for the sake of the parallels, and these can be sustained only by a constant resort to coincidence and improbability.

The second is one close to Tolstoy's heart. In writing the historical sections of his work, he was at great pains to make the settings authentic. But Shakespeare took no such trouble. Anachronisms abound. For example, the setting of *King Lear* is 800 BC, but Shakespeare makes extensive use of details that could have occurred only in the Middle Ages.

The third is that Shakespeare is artificial. Emotion, for example, is overplayed. When a character goes mad he is exhibited centre stage and his ravings are prolonged apparently for their own sake. Death affects his characters in droves, so that by the end of a play the stage is littered with corpses. Language is over-luxuriant, metaphors breeding metaphors in excess of what is required by the dramatic action.

The fourth is also close to Tolstoy's heart. In his own work, he strove to bring his characters alive, distinct in speech and behaviour. Shakespeare's plays seem to lack the first requirement for individuating character in that all his characters speak alike. If his characters differ in speech, says Tolstoy, it is because Shakespeare gives them different speeches, not because they speak differently.

The above criticisms, it seems to me, have a significance which is independent of their own worth; for they throw light on Tolstoy's motives in his whole attack on Shakespeare. Thus it is obvious, from these criticisms, that Tolstoy sees Shakespeare as constantly violating the standards of the art he practises himself. But then it is also obvious, at least on reflection, that he must see the celebration of Shakespeare as the celebration of an art in conflict with his own. That gives his criticism a personal basis. But it is not a petty one. What is at stake, as he sees it, are the standards of that art to which he has devoted much of his life. That in itself should convince the impartial reader of his sincerity.

In the next section, Tolstoy deals with the moral content of Shakespeare's plays. Here he relies heavily on interpretations derived from certain nineteenth-century critics. He was entitled to do so, for they were the leading authorities of his day. Nevertheless the section retains little interest, because, for reasons which we shall consider presently, the critics to whom he refers have lost much of their authority.

As we have seen, Orwell in his criticism of Tolstoy takes for granted that if an artist such as Shakespeare has been celebrated for some three hundred years, it must be futile or even meaningless to deny him merit. Tolstoy now proceeds to answer such criticism. His aim, let it be noted, is the limited one of getting his own criticism heard. His aim, in short, is not to show that Shakespeare is a bad artist but to show that a bad artist *can* become famous and, having become famous, *can* continue to be so.

His argument depends on points which, though obvious on reflection, are often overlooked. First, it should be obvious that fame and merit are not the same. Nor do they necessarily coincide. In addition to having merit there must be other factors which make one famous. These factors will be arbitrary with regard to merit itself. For example, none of the works composed by Aristotle has survived. His fame depends on his lecture notes, which were preserved by his pupils. His pupils might not have preserved them. Or, had they been preserved, like his compositions, they might not have long survived.

But granting that fame and merit are not the same, is it conceivable that the fame of a bad artist can be other than temporary? Yes, it is conceivable, because fame has a tendency to perpetuate itself. Tolstoy illustrates the process with an example that should be familiar to us:

> Since the development of the press it has come about that as soon as something obtains a special significance from accidental circumstances, the organs of the press immediately announce this significance. And as soon as the press has put forward the importance of the matter, the public directs yet more attention to it. The hypnotization of the public incites the press to regard the thing more attentively and in greater detail. The interest of the public is still further increased, and the organs of the press, competing one with another respond to the public demand.[12]

Such crazes, it is true, are usually temporary; but they do not have to be. They will last as long as they answer to an interest and they will last a long time if they answer to a lasting interest.[13]

Tolstoy now moves from the general to the specific, offering to explain the circumstances which account for Shakespeare's fame. He begins by stating that Shakespeare's reputation as a supreme master dates from the end of the eighteenth century. Before that time, he was freely criticized, on grounds very like Tolstoy's own, by the most prominent critics in the language. Here Tolstoy is certainly correct. Dryden, for example, the leading critic of the seventeenth century, wrote of Shakespeare in the following terms:

> it must be allowed to the present age, that the tongue in general is so much refined since Shakespeare's time that many of his words, and more of his phrases, are scarce intelligible. And of those which we understand, some are ungrammatical, others coarse; and his whole style is so pestered with figurative expressions, that it is as affected as it is obscure.[14]

Dr Johnson, the greatest English critic of the eighteenth century, was indeed an admirer of Shakespeare, but he was a highly critical one. 'The style of Shakespeare,' says Johnson, 'was ungrammatical, perplexed and obscure', many passages being 'obscured by obsolete phraseology, or by the writer's unskilfulness and affection'.[15] On the Continent, critics were even more severe. Voltaire, for example, treated Shakespeare as too primitive or barbaric to satisfy civilized taste.

Shakespeare's reputation as the master of all dramatists arose, according to Tolstoy, at the end of the eighteenth century, through the influence of German Romanticism. At the time, drama on the Continent was dominated by the French school, which based its work on the severest principles of Classicism, such as the so-called law of the three unities. Shakespeare's irregularity or barbarism, when judged by those principles, became for the Germans not a vice but a virtue, for they wished to counteract the influence of the French and to develop an art of their own. The leading figure here was Goethe, who was in a position to dictate national taste. His praise for Shakespeare was repeated and exaggerated by innumerable lesser figures. Through the influence of German Romanticism on such critics as Coleridge, Shakespeare soon acquired in his own country the reputation he had already acquired in Germany. In order to illustrate the contrast with previous centuries, Tolstoy now quotes some comments on Shakespeare that were typical of nineteenth-century criticism. The following is an example:

> To Shakespeare the epithet of great applies naturally; and if one adds that independently of his greatness he has also become the reformer of all literature, and moreover has expressed in his works not only the phenomena of the life of his time, but also from thoughts and views that in his day existed only in germ has prophetically foreseen the direction which the social spirit would take in the future (of which we see an amazing example in Hamlet) – one may say without hesitation that Shakespeare was not only a great, but the greatest of all poets that ever existed, and that in the sphere of poetic creation the only rival that equals him is life itself, which in his productions he displayed with such perfection.[16]

Tolstoy spends some time in criticizing the aesthetic principles of German Romanticism. In the course of doing so, he repeats his view, already familiar to us, that the essence of art is religious. But he also defends himself explicitly against the charge of didacticism. We need only quote his words, which make his position entirely clear:

> 'But', I shall be asked, 'what do you mean by the words "religious essence of the drama"? Is not what you demand for the drama religious instruction, didactics: What is called a tendency – which is incompatible with true art?' By 'the religious essence of art', I reply, I mean not an external inculcation of any religious truth in artistic guise, and not an allegorical representation of those truths, but the expression of a definite view of life corresponding to the highest religious understanding of a given period: an outlook which, serving as the impelling motive for the composition of the drama, permeates the whole work though the author be unconscious of it.[17]

## Tolstoy and Shakespeare

On an impartial reading, Tolstoy's criticisms of Shakespeare are not simply sincere but also serious, in the sense that any admirer of Shakespeare should feel the need to answer them. How then should such an admirer respond? A proper answer to that question would take us beyond the scope of this work and would in any case require a competence which I lack. Some points, however, seem clear.

The best Shakespearean critics in the first part of the twentieth century – for example, F. R. Leavis, L. C. Knights and G. Wilson Knight – have not taken the part of Tolstoy's opponents against Tolstoy himself but have rejected the ground they had in common. Such critics have emphasized that Shakespeare's medium is poetic drama, a distinctive form, having its own laws for the development of character and incident, not to be assessed by the standards of nineteenth-century realistic drama or fiction. The point is easily illustrated by contrasting Shakespearean drama with realistic or non-poetic drama as it flourished in the late nineteenth century. There is an obvious disadvantage in realistic drama in that the author is at the mercy of his characters. Thus he can use only such language as people would use in ordinary circumstances. He can, it is true, introduce extreme situations of grief, terror, and so on, but these are precisely the situations in real life where people are at their least eloquent. The realistic novelist does not have this disadvantage, for the overall style of a novel is in its narration, not in its dialogue.[18] The novelist, therefore, has resources of analysis and evaluation which are not available to the realistic dramatist. But what is not available to the realistic dramatist was available to Shakespeare precisely because he was not in that way realistic. When Tolstoy criticized Shakespearean drama, because its characters all speak alike, he was really indicating a strength in the drama, not a weakness. For he was referring in effect to the poetic medium through which Shakespeare expresses his drama. The power of analysis and evaluation which the novelist exercises through explicit comment, Shakespeare could embody in the language his characters spoke. In one sense, this language, in its richness, is less realistic than that of nineteenth-century drama; in another, it is more realistic, for it enabled Shakespeare to express a more profound view of life.

Every commentator mentions Tolstoy's inability to appreciate Shakespeare's power of expression. It is, indeed, a puzzling phenomenon.[19] My own view is that Tolstoy was led by his own linguistic facility into overestimating his ability to read Shakespeare. It is true that his linguistic facility was very great and he was certainly fluent in English. Almost his last act, for example, was to dictate a message in that language. But great poetry exhibits language at its most subtle and complex. One can be fluent in a language and still be incapable of appreciating its poetry. Nor could translation have been of great assistance to Tolstoy; the difficulty in translating great poetry is notorious. In any case, whatever the cause, Tolstoy concentrated in a Shakespearean play on the developments of character and incident, assessing them by the standards of realistic drama or fiction. The trouble is that it is precisely in its language that one finds what is profound in Shakespeare's plays.

There are other points which seem clear. Since poetic drama, like opera, is not immediately realistic, it can tolerate many conventions which likewise are not realistic in any narrow sense. It seems fairly certain, for example, that when Shakespeare gave Kent a disguise unrealistically impenetrable, he was simply relying on a convention of the Elizabethan theatre. Such a convention, once understood, becomes a strength rather than a weakness; for example, it enables a dramatist to provide his characters with vital information without involving them in the complicated procedures by which information is so often obtained in real life. It will be useful to remind ourselves, at this point, that realistic fiction also has its conventions. For example, when a realistic novelist tells us that a certain character lives at a given place, we do not suspend our reading until we have checked whether at that place there really is such a character. In a sense, that is the most unrealistic convention of all. We have to take as true what we know, in the literal sense, to be false. Nor need we conclude, as do some in recent literary theory, that the realistic artist, in effect if not intent, thereby serves to deceive us. The conventions in the various arts, once we have understood them, become the devices by which those arts will show us reality; they are not screens to separate us from the reality we seek. Realistic art, like any other, has its own conventions, but in the hands of a master they can lead us to reality.

We have still to consider the inconsistencies and improbabilities that Tolstoy detects in Shakespeare's plays. It may be important here to remind ourselves that Shakespeare's plays were not intended to be read. It is something of which we may have occasion to remind ourselves only through struggling with Tolstoy's criticism. It is certainly neglected by many critics. Even L. C. Knights, for example, tells us that it is necessary in order to understand Shakespeare that we attend to the 'words on the page'.[20] There were few pages for an Elizabethan audience to attend to. Shakespeare's works were not collected and published until after his death, and he seems to have made no attempt himself to get them published. The movement of attention in reading a play is quite different from that of watching it. In watching it we inevitably move forward with the action. In reading we can move back and forth; we may suspend our reading in the middle, return to the start and search, if we wish, for inconsistencies between the parts. It is noticeable that the improbabilities which Tolstoy detected in the opening of *King Lear* are more evident in reading the play than in seeing it. In the theatre, Lear's behaviour may strike us as arbitrary or unreasonable, but such behaviour is hardly implausible in a monarch. Before we can analyse the scene in close detail, we have moved on to the next one. As Tolstoy himself implied, a work of art exists only in communication, in its being taken as intended. It follows that an inconsistency which no audience would detect, or treat as such, becomes an inconsistency which from the artistic point of view does not exist.

We may clarify the above remarks if we reflect for a moment on what is meant by realistic art. In its understanding of life, a realistic novel may be far less realistic than a fairy tale. It differs from a fairy tale in its method. For example, it would exclude any event which would count as improbable in a factual report or historical account. It is worth noting that the realistic novel and disinterested historical inquiry developed about the same time. Some history in the nineteenth century – Macaulay's for example – has the style and pace of a novel. Some historical novels – Scott's, perhaps – read in stretches as though they were straight history. Both, since they rely on the printed page, presuppose a communication indefinite in time. An error in a historical work, for example, might not be detected for twenty years. The lapse of time would not remove the historian's responsibility for the error. Indeed, by nineteenth-century standards, if we set aside the physical printing of a work, there is hardly an error or inconsistency which, falling outside the intended line of communication, can be deemed for historical or artistic purposes not to exist.

It is evident that Shakespeare was working with very different standards. In the logic of its events, his art is more akin to that of the fairy story than to that of the historian. Thus, for example, he makes no apparent attempt to remove anachronisms. But, further, he did not presuppose a communication indefinite in time. What could not be detected in the course of a performance, or of a performance repeated on relatively few occasions, could be deemed as outside the intended line of communication. This does not mean, let it be emphasized, that his work will not reward prolonged study. What takes a long time to assimilate may simply be complicated, not profound. What can be grasped at once may be so profound that one can reflect on it for the rest of one's life. But prolonged study of Shakespeare's work needs to take into account its presuppositions.

Further presuppositions are revealed the more one reflects on Tolstoy's criticisms. Tolstoy, we may recall, found Shakespeare artificial or extravagant in language and feeling. In responding to this criticism, we may have occasion to note a striking change in national characteristics. From the eighteenth or nineteenth century onwards, the English are portrayed – perhaps caricatured – as reserved in feeling and expression. The Elizabethan English could hardly be described in such terms, even in caricature. It seems they had a relish for strong emotion, openly expressed. A Shakespearean character would not have been expected to go mad discreetly off stage. The audience would have expected him up front, his madness vividly displayed. It seems, also, that they placed no special value on brevity. So long as one stuck to the point, the more one said the better. In short, they had a relish for language, elaborated for its own sake. They seem also to have had a mastery of speech which strikes us, in our own day, as prodigious. Those who are not specialists now have difficulty in following Shakespeare even on the page. The difficulty is due only in part to obsolete language. In greater part it arises from complexity of meaning. An expression may have two or even three meanings, all of them intended. We are bemused when we reflect that Shakespeare was a popular writer, intelligible on a single performance to ordinary people. Indeed it has been denied that this was so. Some have argued that ordinary people did not really follow Shakespeare's plays but went along for the bawdy or slapstick. This seems implausible, since the bawdy, for example, is expressed with the same complexity of language that one finds throughout the plays.

It seems evident, then, that Shakespeare would not have appeared to his contemporaries as at all artificial or extravagant. He had no choice but to work in the conditions available to him. Those conditions, perhaps, were not suitable for what Voltaire would have called civilized taste. But they were certainly suitable for the creation of great poetry.

A response, therefore, is possible to Tolstoy's criticisms. We may note, however, how much can be learned from taking those criticisms seriously.

## Notes

1   See *Recollections and Essays*, London, OUP, 1952, pp. 307–84.
2   See G. Orwell, *Inside the Whale and Other Essays*, Harmondsworth, Penguin, 1981, pp. 101–21.
3   This point has been made by G. H. Von Wright in 'Tolstoi ja taide' (Tolstoy and Art), *Ajatus ja julistus*, Helsinki, WSOY, 1974, pp. 238–60.
4   Orwell, *Inside the Whale and Other Essays*, p. 105.
5   Here is an example of such attempts as he makes. He quotes Tolstoy as saying that Lear 'has no necessity or motive for his abdication'. To this, he replies that such a motive has been made clear in the first scene: he is old and wishes to retire from the cares of the state. In fact what he supplies is not a quotation. He has plainly reformulated Tolstoy's words. For example, Tolstoy speaks of a reason, not a motive. Tolstoy never denies that Lear's act has a motive in Orwell's sense of the term. He states that motive himself in his account of the plot. As is plain in its context, his point is that Lear's act is not *adequately* motivated. There is no *reason* for it in the play. The play, in short, reveals nothing in Lear's character which would make it seem inevitable that he should act in that way. Charity would suggest that Orwell has simply been careless. But that itself is significant. It is evident that he cannot be bothered to give serious consideration to Tolstoy's arguments.
6   Orwell, *Inside the Whale and Other Essays*, p. 106.
7   Ibid., p. 108.
8   Ibid., p. 114.
9   Ibid., p. 118.
10  Ibid., p. 119.
11  George Gibian, *Tolstoy and Shakespeare*, The Hague, Mouton and Co., 1957, p. 10.
12  'Shakespeare and the Drama', p. 367.
13  David Edwards, in a recent work, gives a relevant example: 'it took two hundred years for the United States to recognize the genocide it committed against the native Indians of North America

(a significant and rather obvious historical fact). As we know, until very recently, the Indians were considered to have been the "merciless" aggressors.' *Free to be Human*, Dartington, Green Books Ltd, 1998, p. 40.
14 Quoted in L. C. Knights, *Explorations*, Harmondsworth, Penguin, 1964, p. 20.
15 Ibid., p. 21.
16 'Shakespeare and the Drama', p. 378.
17 Ibid., p. 376.
18 It is noticeable that novelists such as Ivy Compton-Burnett, who write successfully in something akin to the dialogue form, make use of highly formal or stylized speech.
19 There is another puzzling phenomenon, which we have occasion only to mention. This is Tolstoy's inability to appreciate the Christian implications of Shakespeare's art. Indeed these implications seem to me more evident in *King Lear* than in any of Shakespeare's works, with the possible exception of *Measure For Measure* – *King Lear* is irradiated with a purity which, as the work itself demonstrates, is certainly not of this world.
20 Knights, *Explorations*, p. 18.

# Afterword

The reader, it is hoped, may now distinguish the real from the false Tolstoy. The false Tolstoy holds that art is valuable as a means for transferring feelings from the artist to his audience. The value of the art lies in the goodness of the feelings. Only those feelings are good which can appeal even to the most ignorant. In short, the false Tolstoy combines extreme didacticism with the crudest form of expressivism. For him, artistic form is simply a means, valueless in itself, for conveying moral content. The real Tolstoy holds that art is valueless unless its content is given adequate artistic form. Thus form and content cannot ultimately be separated. Art should express what is important in life but it should do so in its own distinctive way. He holds, it is true, that art should be universal in its appeal. He holds, also, that universal art, in his own time, will appeal more readily to the simple than to the sophisticated. But that is because he believes that the sophisticated, in his own time, have become decadent. In short, they have lost contact with what is of permanent value. Tolstoy's appeal to the universal is therefore an appeal to the standards of classical art. Art should appeal to what is of permanent rather than of passing significance.

# Bibliography

Adamson, R., *Fichte*, Edinburgh, Blackwood, 1881.
Barzun, J. (ed.), *The Pleasures of Music*, London, Michael Joseph, 1954.
Barzun, J., *Darwin, Marx and Wagner*, Chicago, Chicago University Press, 1981.
Bayley, J., *Tolstoy and the Novel*, London, Chatto and Windus, 1966.
Bell, C., *Art*, London, Chatto and Windus, 1949.
Benjamin, W., *Illuminations*, London, Pimlico, 1999.
Berlin, I., *Russian Thinkers*, Harmondsworth, Penguin, 1978.
Berlin, I., *The Roots of Romanticism*, London, Chatto and Windus, 1999.
Collingwood, R. G., *The Principles of Art*, Oxford, OUP, 1958.
Edwards, D., *Free to be Human*, Dartington, Green Books Ltd, 1998.
Ellman, R. (ed.), *The Artist as Critic*, London, W. H. Allen, 1970.
Fichte, J. G., *Addresses to the German Nation*, Chicago, Open Court, 1922.
Gibian, G., *Tolstoy and Shakespeare*, The Hague, Mouton and Co., 1957.
Goldman, A. and Sprinchoin, E., *Wagner on Music and Drama*, London, Gollancz, 1970.
Gorky, M., *Tolstoy, Chekhov and Andreev*, Letchworth, The Hogarth Press, 1934.
Haldane, J., 'Form, Meaning and Value: A History of the Philosophy of Architecture', *The Journal of Architecture*, vol. 4, Spring 1999.
Kingsmill, H., *D. H. Lawrence*, London, Methuen, 1938.
Knights, L. C., *Explorations*, Harmondsworth, Penguin, 1964.
Lawrence, D. H., *Selected Critical Writings*, Oxford, OUP, 1998.
Leavis, F. R., *Anna Karenina and Other Essays*, London, Chatto and Windus, 1967.
Lewis, P., 'Collingwood on Art and Fantasy', *Philosophy*, vol. 64, 1989.
Lewis, P., 'Art, the Community's Medicine', *The British Journal of Aesthetics*, vol. 35, no. 3, 1995.
Long, T. R., 'A Selective Defence of Tolstoy's "What is Art"', *Philosophical Writings*, no. 8, Summer 1998.
Magee, B., *The Philosophy of Schopenhauer*, Oxford, OUP, 1997.
Mandelbaum, M., 'Family Resemblances and Generalisation Concerning the Arts', *American Philosophical Quarterly*, vol. 2, 1965.
Maude, A., *The Life of Tolstoy*, Cambridge, CUP, 1953.
Mounce, H. O., *The Two Pragmatisms*, London, Routledge, 1997.
Orwell, G., *Inside the Whale and Other Essays*, Harmondsworth, Penguin, 1981.
Ridley, A., *R. G. Collingwood*, London, Phoenix, 1998.
Sclafani, R., 'Wollheim on Collingwood', *Philosophy*, vol. 51, 1976.

Scruton, R., *The Aesthetics of Music*, Oxford, Clarendon Press, 1997.

Shaw, B., *Shaw's Music: The Complete Musical Criticism of Bernard Shaw, Volume 3: 1893–1950*, London, Bodley Head, 1981.

Spencer, H., *The Man Versus the State*, Harmondsworth, Penguin, 1969.

Tolstoy, L., *What I Believe*, London, The Free Age Press, 1884.

Tolstoy, L., *Recollections and Essays*, London, OUP, 1952.

Tolstoy, L., *What Is Art?*, trans. A. Maude, London, The World Classics, 1955; trans. R. Peavear, Harmondsworth, Penguin, 1995.

Tolstoy, L., *Anna Karenina*, London, Penguin Books, 1978.

Tolstoy, L., *The Kreutzer Sonata and Other Stories*, Harmondsworth, Penguin, 1985.

Troyat, H., *Tolstoy*, London, W. H. Allen, 1968.

Von Wright, G. H., 'Tolstoi ja taide', *Ajatus ja julistus*, Helsinki, WSOY, 1974.

Waugh, E., *A Tourist in Africa*, London, Methuen, 1960.

Wilde, O., *The Artist as Critic*, ed. R. Ellmann, London, W. H. Allen, 1970.

Wilkinson, R., 'Art, Emotion and Expression', in *Philosophical Aesthetics: An Introduction*, ed. O. Hanfling, Oxford, Blackwell, 1992.

Wilson, A. N., *How Can We Know?*, Harmondsworth, Penguin, 1985.

Wilson, A. N., *Tolstoy*, London, Hamish Hamilton, 1988.

Winters, Y., *In Defence of Reason*, Denver, Swallow Press, 1947.

Winters, Y., *Uncollected Essays and Reviews*, London, Allen Lane, 1974.

Wittgenstein, L., *Philosophical Investigations*, Oxford, Blackwell, 1976.

# Index

action, moral 51
activities, artistic 27
    cost and labour 18
    role in human life 23, 27
Aeschylus 53
alienation effect 18–19, 56
amusement 68
anachronisms in Shakespeare 100, 105
angry child example 68–9, 84
apperceptive mass 8
architecture 93 n12
aria 57, 58, 60
aristocrats 5
Aristotle 85, 91, 101
art,
    abstract 81
    aim of 36
    amusement 83, 88, 90
    and life 79, 82
    and morality 29–33
    and society 34–9
    as expression of artist's feelings 84
    as form of communication 16, 24, 33
    central features 25
    classical 73, 85
    counterfeit 43, 44, 46, 56
    for art's sake 15–16, 77–82, 83, 92
    function of 19, 26
    genuine 43, 44, 46
    Greek 36
    high and low 15–17
    imitative 44
    magic 83, 90
    medieval 29
    moral evaluation of 27–8
    of the future 74–5
    of the people 17
    relationship between producer and receiver 24
    religious 72
    representational 81, 82, 83, 88
    Romantic 40, 47
    schools 19
    sophisticated 15–17, 35
    standards of 100, 108
    theories of 76–92; didactic 76, 77, 79, 82; hedonistic 76, 77; moralistic 76; romantic 76, 77, 82–92
    Tolstoy's definition 23
    true 35
    universal 72–4, 108
art/craft dichotomy 82–9, 93 n12
artist(s) 90
    and ball of clay example 86
    emphasis on 77, 88
    genuine 47
    intentions of 66
    role of 13–14, 38, 75, 83
    sophisticated 39, 42
    training of 46–7
attitude 2
audience 46, 86, 89, 90, 91

Bacon, Francis 71, 72
Bakunin 49
Barzun, Jacques 63
Baudelaire, Charles 41
bawdy 106
Bayley, John: *Tolstoy and the Novel* 46
Bayreuth 50, 54
beauty 19, 20, 23, 34, 36, 40, 74, 78
Beethoven 13, 14, 49
    Third Symphony, the 'Eroica' 44
Behis, Sonya 5–6, 11
Bell, Clive 77, 79–82, 83
    *Art* 80
Berlin, Isaiah 4
Berlioz 13, 44
Bizet's *Carmen* 60
borrowing 43
bourgeoisie 5
boy and wolf example 2, 24–5, 65
boxing 87
Britain 77, 79
Bruckner's Ninth Symphony 32
Bryulóv 47
Buddhism 34
Burns 20

Catholic Church 36, 50
Catholicism 29
Cézanne 79

Chaliapin 16
Chekhov 2, 12 n5
   *Darling* 2–3
Chinese 34
Christianity 34, 36, 38, 60, 72, 75
   of the Gospels 7–10
   Orthodox 7–9
   purification of 37
cinema 46, 60
city dweller 41
Classicism 102
Coleridge 13, 102
collaborator, audience role of 89
Collingwood, R. G. 82–91
   *The Principles of Art* 83, 89
   use of term magic 83
comedian 90
complexity 35, 90, 106
Compton-Burnett, Ivy 107 n18
conditions,
   necessary and sufficient 81
   social 41
consciousness, abnormal states of 63
consumption 36
contemplation 54, 55, 62
content,
   moral 2, 31, 100, 108
   paraphrasable 2, 30
conventions 104
craftsman, role of 13–14
Crane, Hart 63
   *The Dance* 63
critics, place of 46
culture
   of the peasants 16, 42
   of the Russian people 16
   traditional 74, 75
   universal 42

decadence 17, 35, 36, 37, 40–49, 74
   appeal of 43
   distinctive features 40, 42
   four devices 43–6
definitions 21
de Lucia, Fernando 59
De Quincey, Thomas 57, 70
desire 54, 55
Dewey, John 89
Dickens 15
didactic theory 94
didacticism 2, 32, 41, 44, 102, 108

discipline 85, 87
drama,
   poetic 103, 104
   realistic 103, 104
Dresden, revolution in 49, 54
Dryden 101

Elizabethan theatre 104
emotion 79, 80, 84, 91, 100
emotional reaction 63
Enlightenment 3, 4, 6, 7, 8, 37, 38, 50
excitement, audience 63
expression, artistic 90
expressiveness 68, 70, 74
expressivism 108

faith 6
falsification 72, 90
fame and merit 101
feeling 62, 65, 66, 90, 105
Fet 97
Fichte, Johann Gottlieb 51, 52
fiction, realistic 104
folk song 15, 16
form,
   aesthetic 46
   and content 30–32, 65, 108
   artistic 79, 85
   common 45
   significant 80
France 19
French Encyclopaedists 3
French Revolution 14, 37, 38, 49
Frith 80
Fry, Roger 77, 79
function,
   expressive 82, 85
   representative 91

games 21, 81
Gauguin 79
Gautier, Théophile 15–16, 19, 40
   *Mademoiselle de Maupin* 15
Genesis 34
Germany 102
Gibian, George 98
Goethe 14, 102
goodness 36, 41
Gorky 3
Gospels 34, 41, 61, 97
Greeks 34, 35, 51, 53

happiness, symbol for 91
Haydn 85
Hebrews 34
Hegel 51
Heidegger, Martin 52
history 105

Idealism, German 54
imitation 43–4
Impressionists 42, 79
Industrial Revolution 14
industrialization 37, 38, 74
infection 24, 25, 27, 29, 33, 91
'infectiousness' 2, 31, 65–7
intelligence, active 62, 63
intellectuals 5, 49
integration 58, 60
Italy 15

James, William 8
Johnson, Dr 86, 101
Joseph, story of 73–4, 86
judgement, artistic 71

Kant 51, 52
   *Critique of Pure Reason* 51
Knight, G. Wilson 103
Knights, L. C. 103, 104

*laissez-faire* 38
Lawrence, D. H. 1, 12 n11
Leavis, F. R. 103
leitmotif 58
Leonardo 70
Leonardo's *I Pagliacci* 60
Liszt 13, 44, 54
literature 68, 87
Long, Todd 29, 30, 32

Macaulay 105
Magee, Bryan 61
Mahler's Tenth Symphony 32
Mandelbaum, Maurice 22
marriage 9–10
Marx 14
Mascagni's *Cavalleria Rusticana* 60
Maupassant 3, 31, 70
   *Une Partie de Campagne* 31
means and ends 83, 86, 89, 90
medium, artistic 84, 88
Melchior, Lauritz 58

merit, aesthetic 20
Middle Ages 35, 72, 100
Mona Lisa 70
Monet 42
morality 78
moralizing 2, 10
Mozart 13
music 68, 69, 78, 88, 89, 90
   crisis in 45
   genuine 45
   symphonic 15
mystification 3, 4, 7

Nekrasov 5
New Orleans funerals 69
nominalism 85, 86
non-violence 10
North America, native Indians 106–7 n13
noumenal, the 62
novel,
   historical 105
   naturalistic 43
   realistic 94, 105
novelist, realistic 103

obscurity 41, 46
Olivier, Laurence 87
opera 15, 18, 45, 53, 56–60, 104
orchestra, development of 45, 59
orchestration, Wagnerian 73
originality 47, 56
ornamentation 74
Orthodox faith 7
Orwell, George vii, 94–102
   essay 'Lear, Tolstoy and the Fool' 94–102
Owen, Wilfred 92

*Paddington Station* 80
painting 68, 74
paraphrase 30, 32
particularity 84–5
peasant(s) 5, 16, 41
phenomenal, the 62
philosophers of aesthetics 19, 20, 23
photography 14, 80, 81, 82
Pissarro 42
Plato 27, 51
   letters 51
   *Phaedrus* 51
   *Symposium* 51

pleasure, aim of art 27, 34, 35, 76
plots 46
poetry 83, 87, 88, 92, 103, 106
Post-Impressionists 79
priests 3
professionalism in the arts 46
progressive religion 4
propaganda, distinction between art and 90
Protestants 36, 37
Psalms 34
pseudo art 80
Puccini
   *La Bohème* 60
   *Tosca* 60

raw material 83, 87
reading, aloud and silently, example 66–7, 69
realism 31
reason 3, 6, 51, 52
recitative 57, 58, 60
Reformation, Protestant 37, 52
regeneration, moral 52, 53
Rembrandt 81, 82
Renoir 42
representation 69, 70, 82
resemblance(s) 21–2, 69, 70, 88
Ridley, Aaron 88
Rimbaud, Arthur 63
Roman Empire 34, 36, 60
Romans 34, 35
Romanticism, German 102
Romantic movement 77, 86
Romantic period 13, 45, 51
Rousseau 5
Russian language 20

sacraments 7
Saint-Saëns 59
scepticism 35, 37, 67
Schnorr, Ludwig 60
Schopenhauer, Arthur 54, 55, 61, 62
Schubert 15
scientific positivists 51
Scott 105
Scruton, Roger 70
Second World War 38
self-expression 77
sense experience 51
sentimentality 31
sex 46

Shakespeare 20, 62, 66, 67, 78, 89, 94–107
   Christian implications 107 n19
   *Hamlet* 78, 89, 99
   *King Lear* 20, 94–107; Cordelia 98, 99; Gloucester 100; Kent 98, 99, 104
   *Macbeth* 62, 66, 85
   *Measure for Measure* 107 n19
   *Othello* 99; Desdemona 99; Iago 99
Shaw, Bernard 60
simplicity 34, 36, 63
sin 50, 51
sincerity 46, 65, 66, 67, 92, 100
slapstick 106
sonnet 30
speculative metaphysics 51
speech 26
Spencer, Herbert 37
Spinoza 51
spirit 52, 54
spontaneity 86, 87
St Paul 50
Stendhal 5
   *The Charterhouse of Parma* 5
Stravinsky 16
   *The Rite of Spring* 16
striking device 44–6
striking effects 59
subject matter 32, 41, 42, 44, 65, 70, 78
subjectivism 84
success, criterion 39
suffering 5
symbol(s) 78, 79, 91

talent 43
themes, universality of 74, 86
Tolstoy,
   and education 5
   attitude to miracles 8
   behaviour in controversy 40
   commandments 8–9
   criticism of Wagner 55–64
   diaries 97
   dislike of Shakespeare 98
   essay 'Shakespeare and The Drama' 94–107; anachronisms 100; improbabilities of characterization 98, 99–10; inconsistencies 104–5; language 105–6; overplayed emotion 100, 105; reason for Shakespeare's fame 101–2

fluency in English 103–4
marriage 5, 11
real and false 108
religious conversion 1, 97
resemblances between Lear and Tolstoy 95–6
shorter works 12 n5
spiritual crisis 6
spiritual pride 96–7
study of the Gospels 7
view of art 46
*What is Art?*; choice of examples 74; eighth to fifteenth chapters 40; eleventh chapter 43; fifteenth chapter 65; fifth chapter 24; first chapter 68; fourth chapter 20; nineteenth chapter 74; second chapter 19; sixteenth chapter 65, 74; tenth chapter 43; third chapter 20
works,
    *A Confession* 1, 6; *After the Ball* 1; *Anna Karenina* 1, 5, 6, 44, 65; *Childhood* 4, 5; essay on Maupassant 31; *Father Sergius*1, 97; *Hadji Murat* 1, 10–11; *Master and Man* 1; *Resurrection* 1, 5; *Sevastopol Sketches* 5; *The Death of Ivan Ilyich* 1; *The Devil* 1; *The Forged Coupon* 1; *The Kreutzer Sonata* 1, 9; *War and Peace* 1, 5, 6
Tolstoy, Nicholas (father and brother) 4
treatment, artistic 77, 78, 82

Troyat, Henri 2, 11
Turgenev 5, 97

*Uncle Tom's Cabin* 2
upper classes 35, 36

Van Gogh 79
Verdi 60
*Volga Boat Song* 16
Volkonsky, Prince 3, 4
Voltaire 7, 101, 106
voluntarism 37

Wagner, Richard 47, 49–64
    influences on 50–51
    prose writings 50, 59
    works, *Die Valküre* 58; *Lohengrin* 49; *Tannhäuser* 49; *The Flying Dutchman* 49; *The Ring of the Nibelungen* 50, 55, 58; *Tristan and Isolde* 50, 61–3
warfare 5
Waugh, Evelyn 71, 72
Welsh and British example 81
Wilde, Oscar 16, 77, 78, 79, 80, 82
    *The Picture of Dorian Gray* 77, 78
Wilkinson, Robert 25, 29, 32
Wilson, A. N. 12 n5
Winters, Yvor 63, 76, 77
Wittgenstein 21–2, 23
    *Philosophical Investigations* 21
Wordsworth 13

Yasnaya Polyana 3

For Product Safety Concerns and Information please contact our EU
representative GPSR@taylorandfrancis.com
Taylor & Francis Verlag GmbH, Kaufingerstraße 24, 80331 München, Germany

www.ingramcontent.com/pod-product-compliance
Lightning Source LLC
Chambersburg PA
CBHW071407290426
44108CB00014B/1717